150 CROCHET TRIMS

150 CROCHET TRIMS

Designs for beautiful decorative edgings,
from lacy borders to bobbles, braids,
and fringes

Susan Smith

St. Martin's Griffin
New York

Library of Congress Cataloging-in-Publication Data Available
Upon Request

ISBN-10: 0-312-35982-9
ISBN-13: 978-0-312-35982-9

First published in the United States by St. Martin's Griffin

First U.S. Edition: April 2007
Conceived, designed and produced by
Quarto Publishing plc
The Old Brewery
6 Blundell Street
London N7 9BH

QUAR: CTR

Project Editor: Lindsay Kaubi
Art Editor: Jacqueline Palmer
Designer: Susi Martin
Assistant Art Director: Penny Cobb
Illustrator: Coral Mula
Pattern Checker: Helen Jordan
Photographers: Phil Wilkins and Paul Forrester
Proofreader: Christine Vaughan
Indexer: Diana LeCore

Art Director: Moira Clinch
Publisher: Paul Carslake

Manufactured by Modern Age Repro House Ltd., Hong Kong
Printed by SNP Leefung printers Ltd., China

10 9 8 7 6 5 4 3 2 1

CONTENTS

AUTHOR'S FOREWORD

I am extremely passionate about crafts and have been crocheting for as long as I can remember. For me, creating something is as much about enjoying the journey as it is about the final product. I believe that any item that is hand crafted is a unique creation to be treasured.

This book is not only for those with lots of crochet experience but also for beginners. The vast, diverse, and beautiful selection of crochet trims featured in this book range from the very easy to make to the complex and challenging; however, the nature of the book allows anyone—no matter how experienced or inexperienced a crocheter—to embellish an item with a decorative trim. Hopefully this book will also encourage readers to start creating and designing their own crochet work.

Susan Smith

ABOUT THIS BOOK

The book begins with a stunning visual directory of 150 crochet trims: once you've chosen the trim you'd like to make, use the handy trim reference number to locate its pattern in the Technical Data chapter. In the Projects chapter you will discover five inspirational project ideas for using and applying the trims. At the end of the book the Refresher Course contains all the basic information and crochet skills needed to work all the trims in the book: all techniques are clearly explained with step-by-step instructions and illustrations.

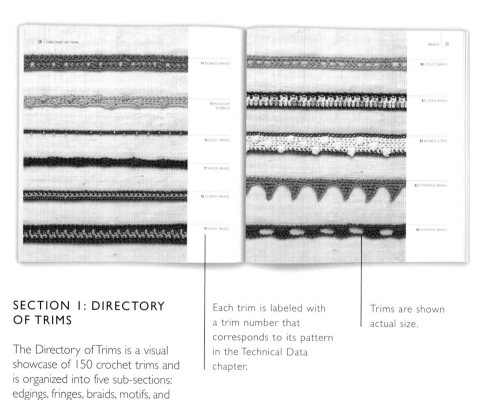

SECTION 1: DIRECTORY OF TRIMS

The Directory of Trims is a visual showcase of 150 crochet trims and is organized into five sub-sections: edgings, fringes, braids, motifs, and accessories. Each trim is displayed actual size—just flick through and pick your trim.

Each trim is labeled with a trim number that corresponds to its pattern in the Technical Data chapter.

Trims are shown actual size.

SECTION 2: TECHNICAL DATA

Here, you'll find the patterns for every single trim along with information on the yarns, beads, and sequins used to make each trim. There is also a detailed picture of each trim, going in closer than the directory so that you can see the stitches in detail. The Technical Data section is also organized into the five trim sections and each trim is labeled with its trim number as well as a page reference telling you where it is in the directory.

SECTION 3: PROJECTS

There are five attractive and inspirational projects ranging from a beret embellished with a floral motif to a silky cushion with a funky textured fringe. All of the projects are designed to encourage you to try using the trims in the book and to experiment with varying the colors, textures, beads, and sequins used.

Each pattern appears in full.

Every trim pattern is rated according to skill level: beginner/easy, intermediate, or challenging/complex.

Use the trim number to refer back to the actual size trim photograph in the directory.

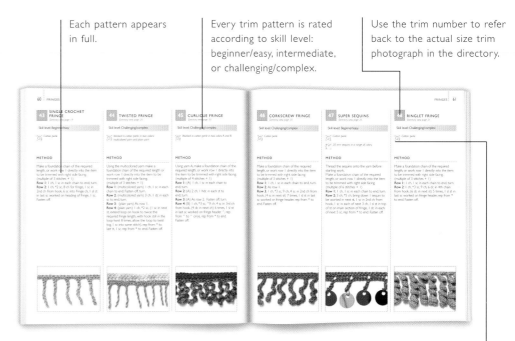

Instructions list the trims used, the materials needed, and how to make and attach the trim.

Each project is illustrated with an inspirational picture of the finished item.

UNDERSTANDING THE SYMBOLS

Each trim pattern is accompanied by one or two symbols indicating the materials needed and, in some cases, the application for the trim.

Yarn used

Bead, sequin, or finding used

Application/use for trim.

SECTION 4: REFRESHER COURSE

The Refresher Course guides you step-by-step through all the crochet basics in easy to follow sequences: from choosing a hook and yarn and basic stitches to working textured stitches and three-dimensional motifs.

DIRECTORY OF TRIMS

Most of us have something to which we'd like to add a personal touch: clothing bought impulsively; an old favorite that needs a new lease of life, or maybe a plain piece of knitting or crochet that would be beautifully complemented with a trim. Explore this stunning visual directory of 150 crocheted edgings, fringes, braids, motifs, and accessories and you're sure to find the trim to suit you. Each beautifully photographed trim is displayed actual size and labeled with a trim number that corresponds to its pattern in the Technical Data chapter (pages 46–97), so that once you've chosen your trim you can flip directly to the pattern.

EDGINGS

Crochet edgings attached to a hem or seam can be used to fantastic effect to complement a fabric garment or soft furnishing. Edgings can be used on their own but can also be used in groups where they can interact visually to create interesting and textural patterns (see pages 106–107).

TO MAKE:

For edging patterns, see pages 48–57

1 SHELL EDGE

2 SCALLOP EDGE

3 GLITZY EDGE

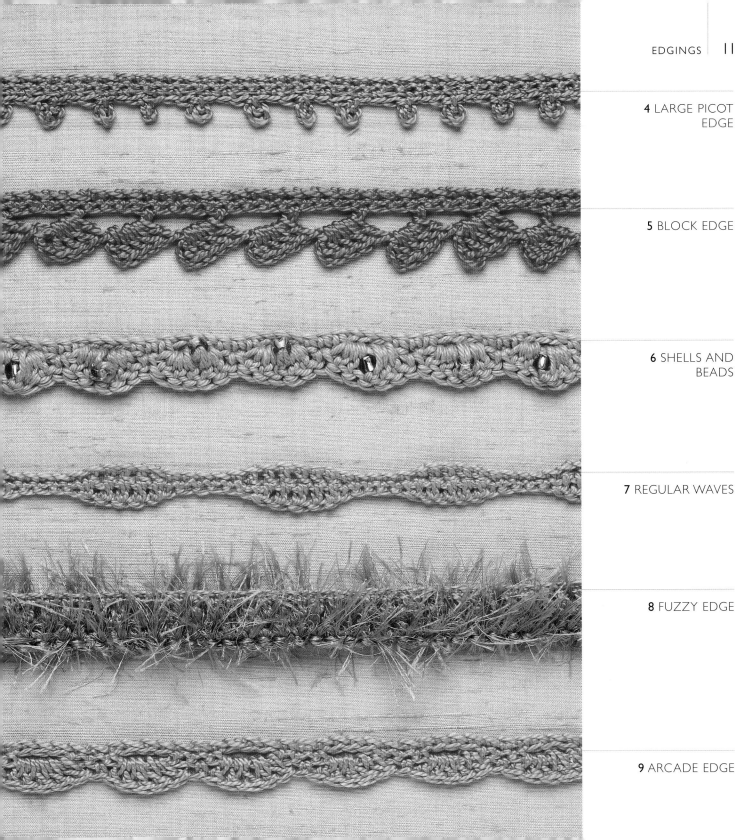

4 LARGE PICOT EDGE

5 BLOCK EDGE

6 SHELLS AND BEADS

7 REGULAR WAVES

8 FUZZY EDGE

9 ARCADE EDGE

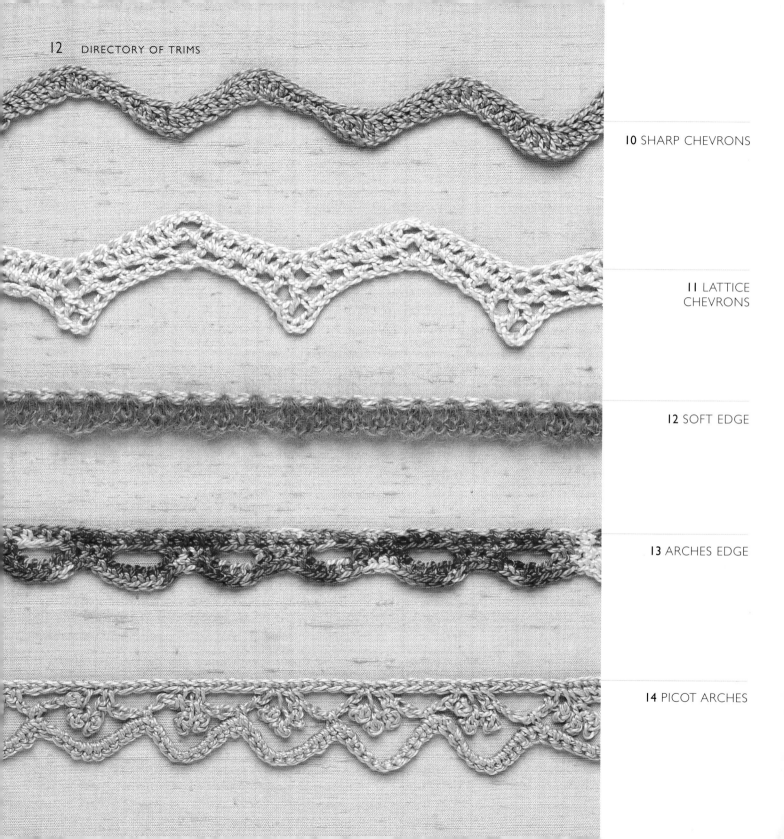

10 SHARP CHEVRONS

11 LATTICE
CHEVRONS

12 SOFT EDGE

13 ARCHES EDGE

14 PICOT ARCHES

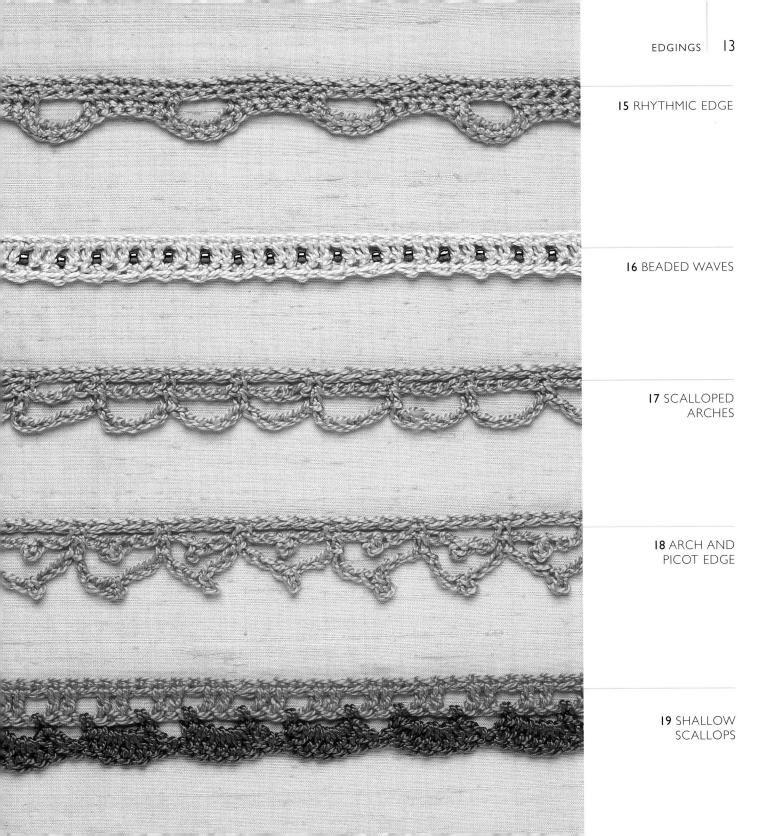

15 RHYTHMIC EDGE

16 BEADED WAVES

17 SCALLOPED
ARCHES

18 ARCH AND
PICOT EDGE

19 SHALLOW
SCALLOPS

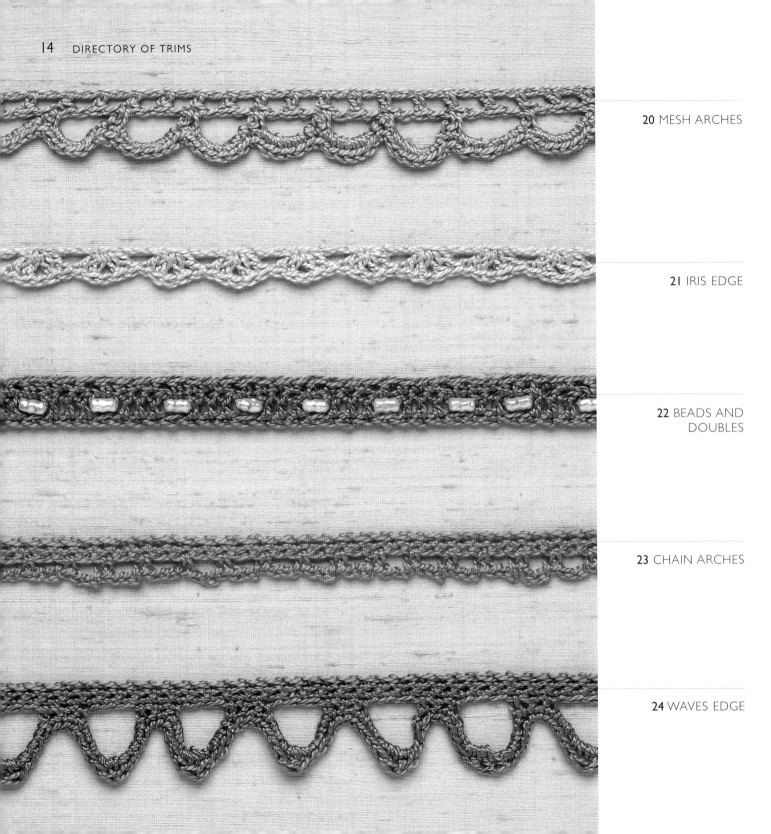

20 MESH ARCHES

21 IRIS EDGE

22 BEADS AND
DOUBLES

23 CHAIN ARCHES

24 WAVES EDGE

25 LAYERED CHAINS

26 SIMPLY BEADS

27 FLORAL EDGE

28 POSY EDGE

29 IRIS STITCH EDGE

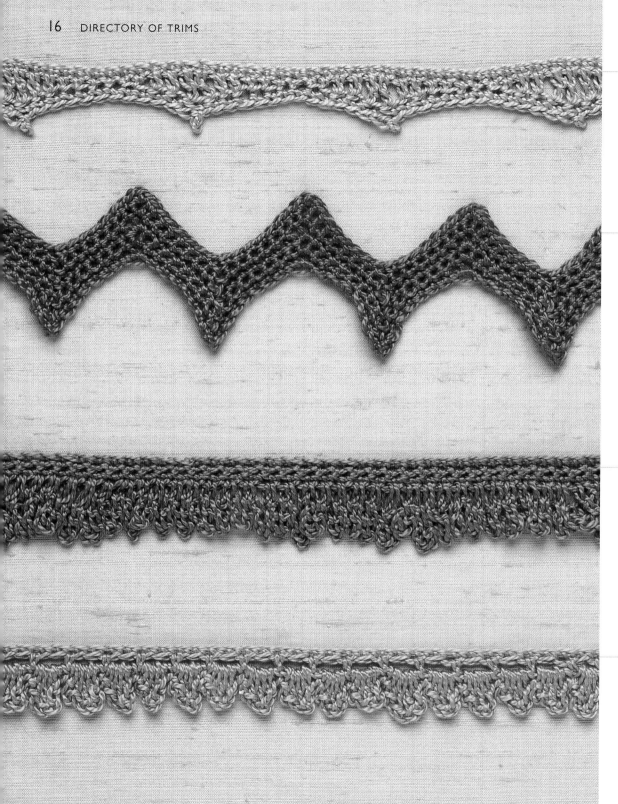

30 UNDULATING EDGE

31 INTERLACED EDGE

32 DEEP RIPPLES

33 SHALLOW RIPPLES

34 FRILLY EDGE

35 SURFACE BLOCKS

36 PARALLEL LINES

37 FRILLED EDGING

FRINGES

A crocheted fringe is a fun way to add a touch of glamour and movement to a plain knitted or crocheted garment. Here you'll find fringes in a range of yarn types from fine and delicate to thick and chunky. There are also examples using novelty yarns, beads, and sequins in ways that won't overwhelm the look of the original piece.

TO MAKE:

For fringe patterns, see pages 58–66

38 BEADED FILET FRINGE

39 TRIPLE LOOP FRINGE

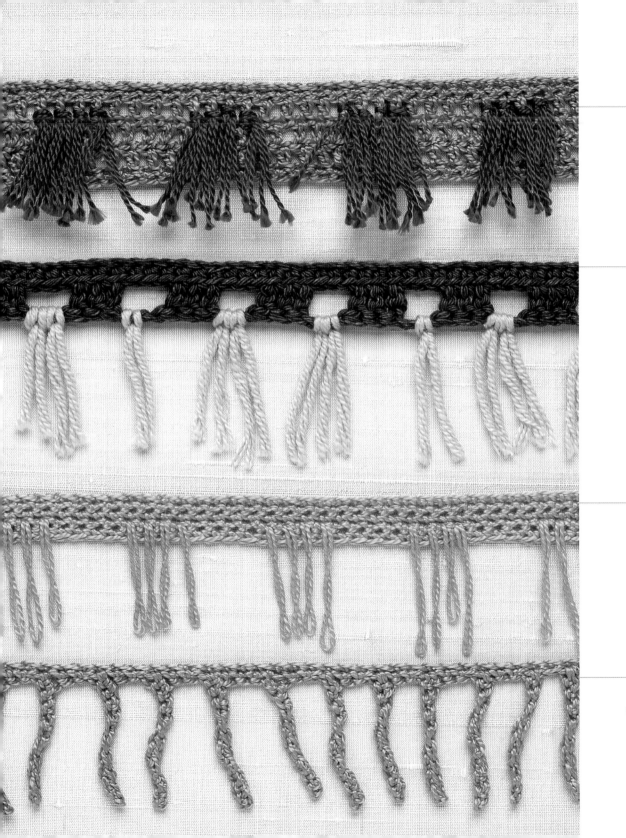

40 BLOCK FRINGE

41 OPEN BLOCK
FRINGE

42 RANDOM
FRINGE

43 SINGLE
CROCHET FRINGE

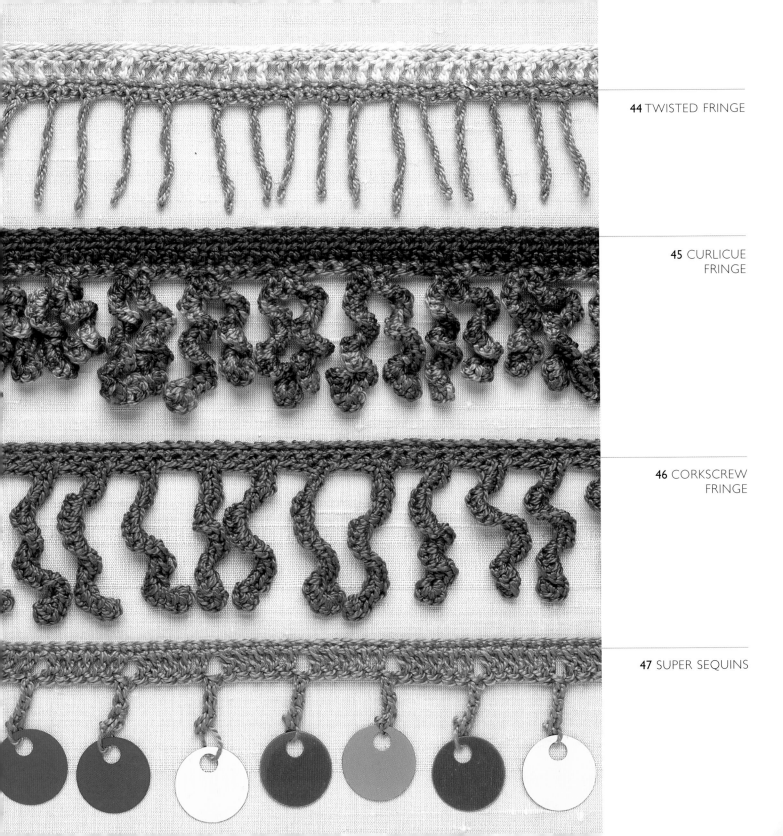

44 TWISTED FRINGE

45 CURLICUE FRINGE

46 CORKSCREW FRINGE

47 SUPER SEQUINS

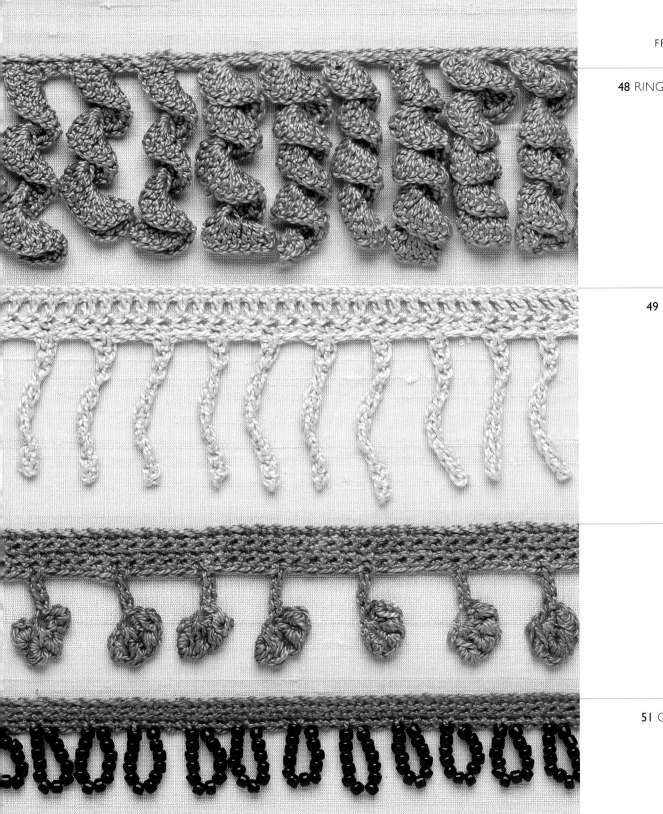

48 RINGLET FRINGE

49 SLIP FRINGE

50 TWISTED BULLIONS

51 ONLY BEADS

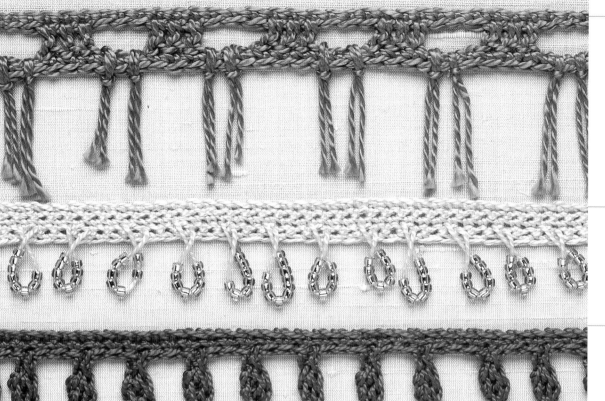

52 LATTICE FRINGE

53 PARTLY BEADS

54 UNDULATING FRINGE

55 EYELASH FRINGE

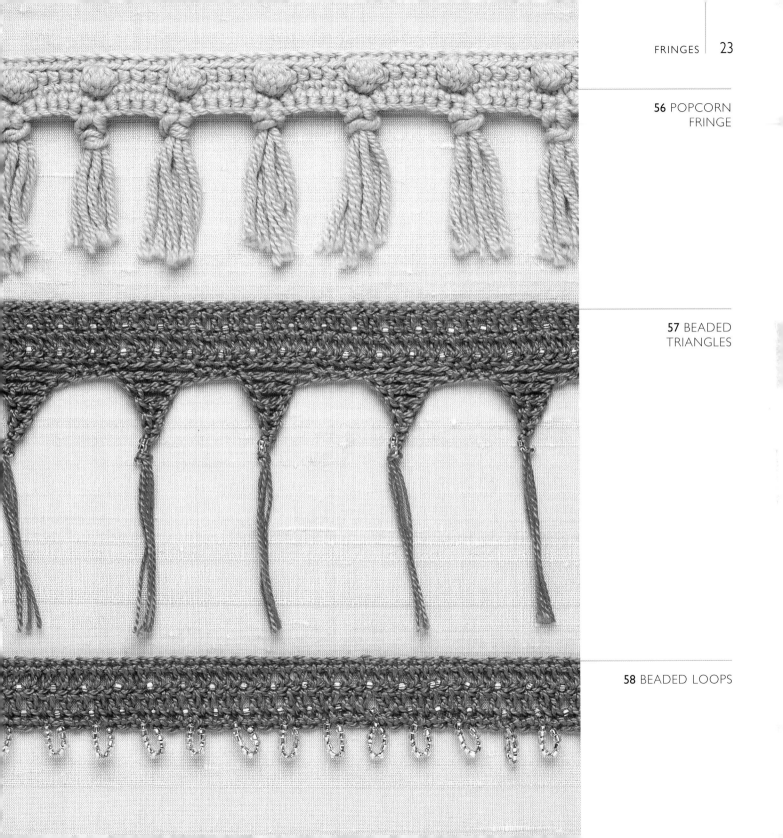

56 POPCORN
FRINGE

57 BEADED
TRIANGLES

58 BEADED LOOPS

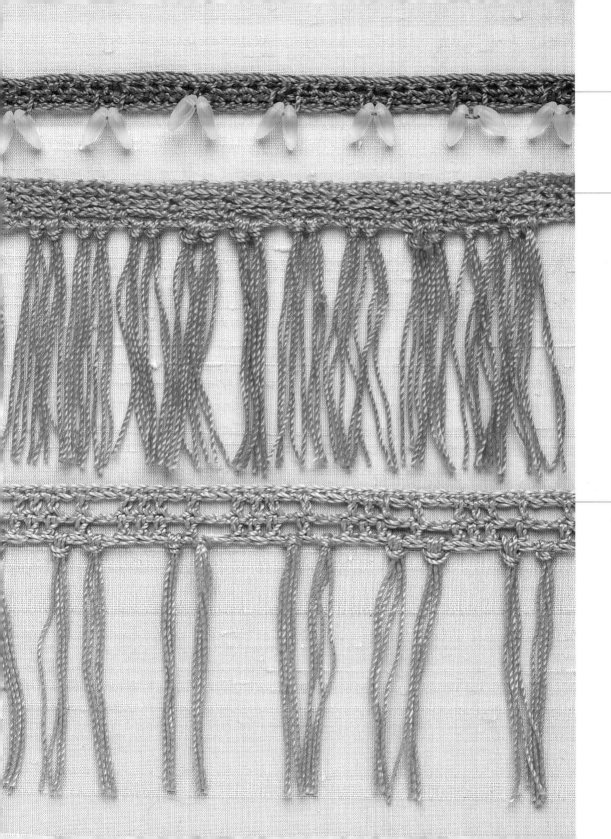

61 PEARL LEAF
FRINGE

62 DOUBLE MESH
FRINGE

63 GRANNY FRINGE

BRAIDS

Whether you want a braid with bobbles, waves, sequins, beads, chevrons, or stripes there's a huge range to choose from in this section. Versatile braids can be delicately stitched to a garment or firmly glued to soft furnishings, adding fine and detailed decoration.

TO MAKE:

For braid patterns, see pages 67–73

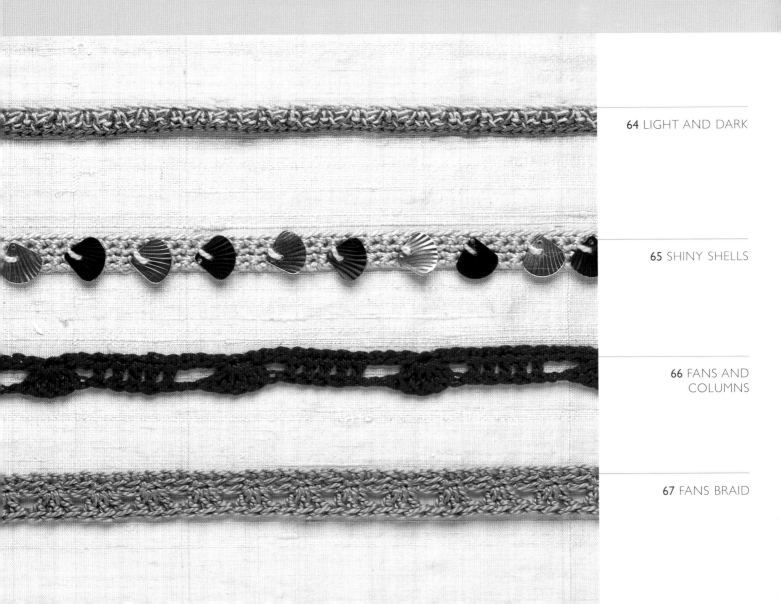

64 LIGHT AND DARK

65 SHINY SHELLS

66 FANS AND COLUMNS

67 FANS BRAID

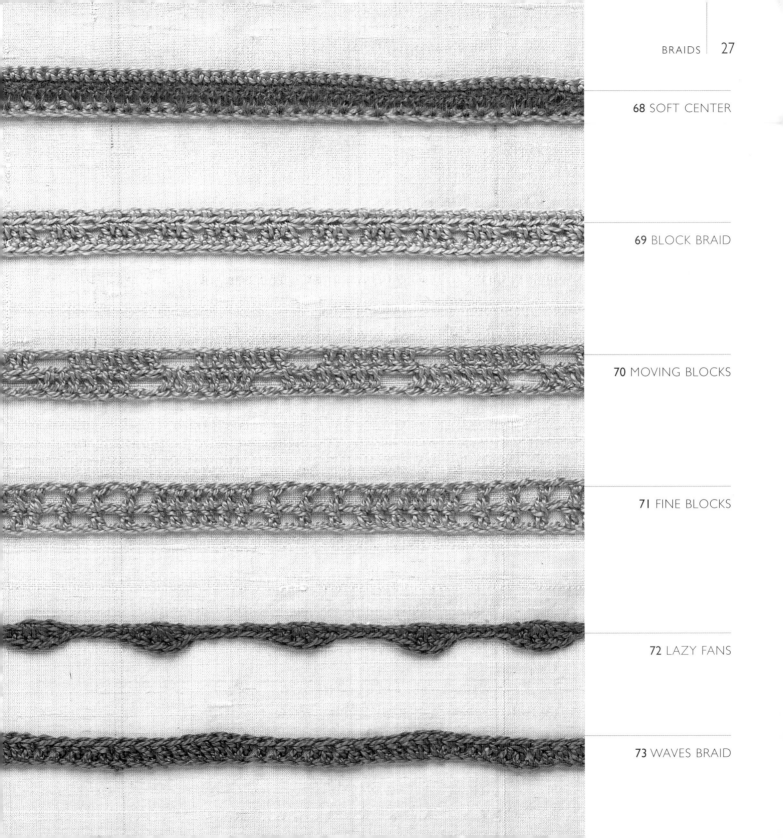

68 SOFT CENTER

69 BLOCK BRAID

70 MOVING BLOCKS

71 FINE BLOCKS

72 LAZY FANS

73 WAVES BRAID

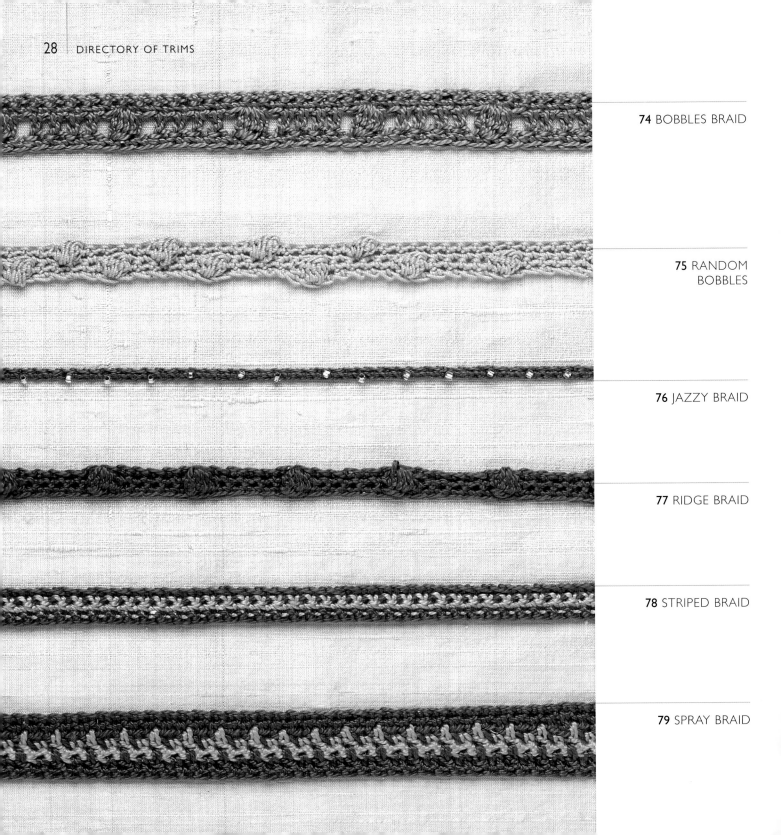

74 BOBBLES BRAID

75 RANDOM BOBBLES

76 JAZZY BRAID

77 RIDGE BRAID

78 STRIPED BRAID

79 SPRAY BRAID

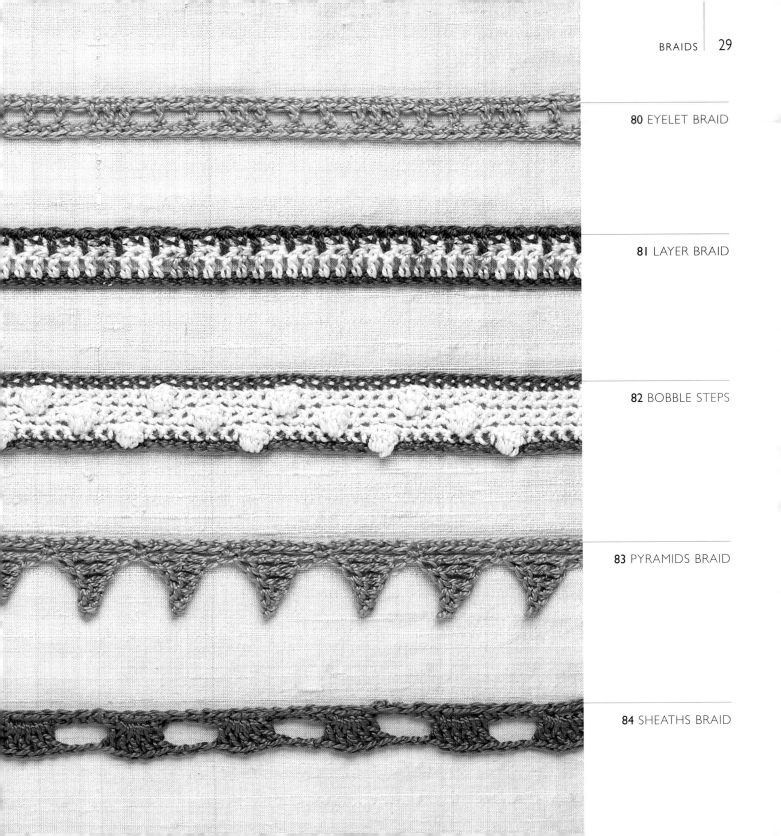

80 EYELET BRAID

81 LAYER BRAID

82 BOBBLE STEPS

83 PYRAMIDS BRAID

84 SHEATHS BRAID

85 LONG WAVES

86 ANGLED
CHEVRONS

87 SHALLOW FILET
BRAID

88 DEEP FILET
BRAID

89 LUXURIOUS
BRAID

MOTIFS

Fashionable and versatile, crocheted motifs can be attached to a brooch back to pin to your favorite jacket or hat, sewn to a silky cushion, or added to a blank greetings card for a special occasion. Incorporating many themes, including flowers, leaves, and snowflakes, these exciting decorations can take the form of simple silhouettes or three-dimensional, bead-embellished bouquets.

TO MAKE:

For motif patterns, see pages 74–86

90 SUN DAISY

91 GOLDEN PANSY

92 SUNBURST

93 CLOVER

94 IRISH SHAMROCK

95 LINKED PETALS

96 SUNSHINE

97 ENGLISH ROSE

98 IRISH LEAF

99 PRINCELY PETALS

100 FAN CIRCLE

101 SILHOUETTE
CLOVER

102 WESTERN
MOTIF

103 LAYERED ROSE

104 ELEGANT ROSE

105 FLOWER
SILHOUETTE

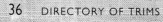

110 TRELLIS MOTIF

111 MARIGOLD

112 STAR FLOWER

113 CIRCLED LACE

114 FRAMED FLOWER

115 SQUARE FRAMED CIRCLES

116 PINWHEEL

117 CHRYSANTHEMUM

118 CHAIN FLOWER

119 GOLDEN LEAF

120 LAZY FROG

121 TUFTED
FLOWER

122 CONICAL SHELL

123 PEARL ROSE

124 SNOWFLAKE

ACCESSORIES

The accessories included in this directory are decorative but functional crocheted items, that will not only add visual interest to a garment but also serve a purpose. On the next few pages you 'll find chunky crochet-covered buttons, decorative buttonholes, floral collars, lacy insertions, and tasseled and beaded belt ties.

TO MAKE:

For accessory patterns, see pages 87–97

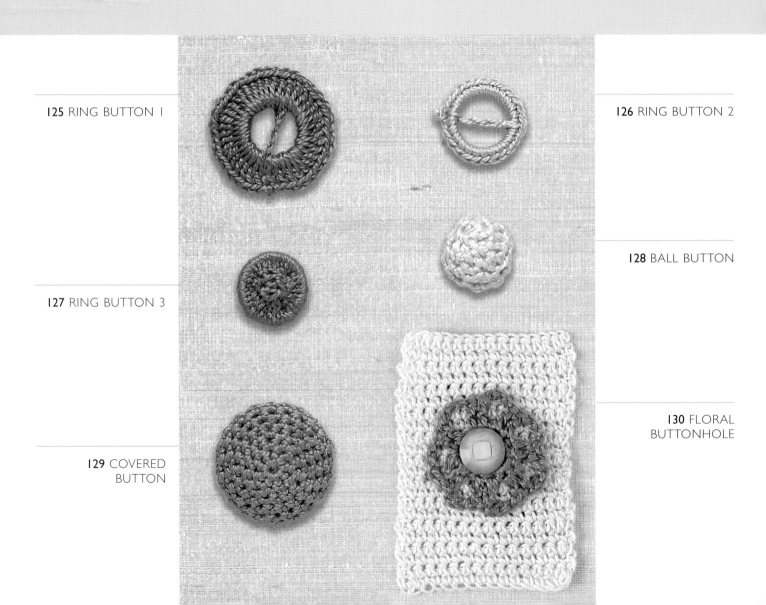

125 RING BUTTON I

126 RING BUTTON 2

127 RING BUTTON 3

128 BALL BUTTON

129 COVERED BUTTON

130 FLORAL BUTTONHOLE

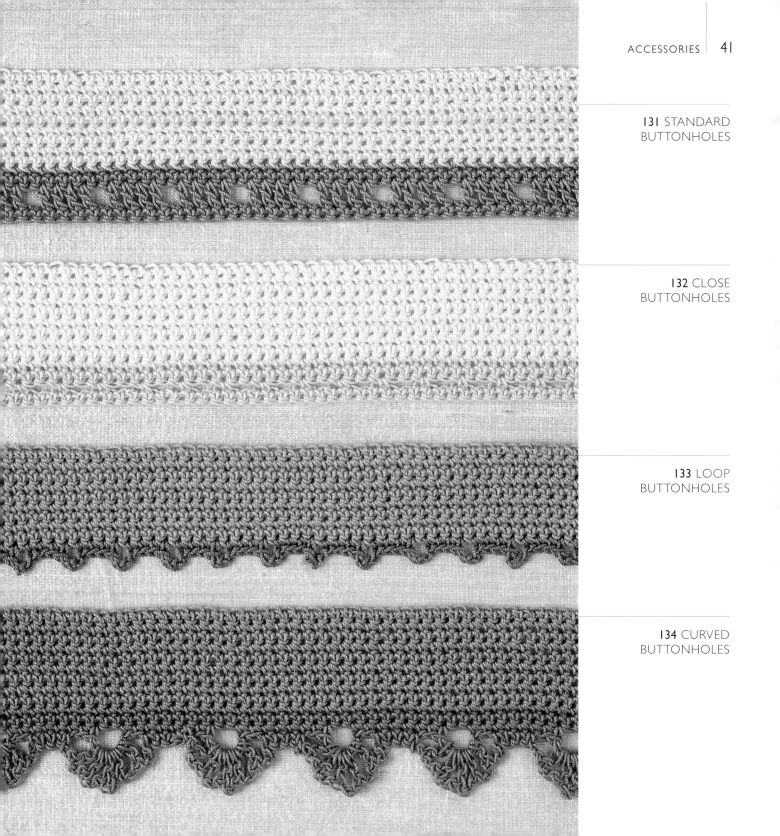

131 STANDARD
BUTTONHOLES

132 CLOSE
BUTTONHOLES

133 LOOP
BUTTONHOLES

134 CURVED
BUTTONHOLES

135 LOOPED PICOT
BUTTONHOLES

136 PICOT
BUTTONHOLES

137 TEXTURED
RUFFLE

138 DIAMONDS
INSERTION

139 DECORATIVE CUFF

140 COLUMNS INSERTION

141 SPIKED COLUMNS INSERTION

142 MINI CIRCLES INSERTION

143 BASIC COLLAR

144 LACE COLLAR

145 INTRICATE LACE
COLLAR

146 FAN COLLAR

147 PICOT COLLAR

TECHNICAL DATA

This chapter contains all the information you need to make the
trims in the directory. Each crochet pattern is accompanied by a list
of the materials needed, and a page reference and trim number to
guide you to its position in the directory. There is also a detailed
photograph of the trim so that you can see the stitches.

EDGINGS

SEE ALSO

*Standard crochet abbreviations,
page 125
Refresher course,
pages 110–125*

SHELL EDGE
Directory view, page 10

Skill level: Beginner/easy

*Worked in cotton perle in
two colors: A and B*

METHOD

Using color A, make a foundation chain of the required length, or work row 1 directly into the item to be trimmed with right side facing. (multiple of 6 stitches + 1)
Row 1: (A) 1ch, 1sc in each st or position to end, turn.
Row 2: (A) As row 1.
Row 3: (A) As row 1. Fasten off.
Row 4: Join in color B. 1 ch, *skip 2 sc, 5 dc in next sc, skip 2 sts, 1sc in next st, rep from * to end. Fasten off.

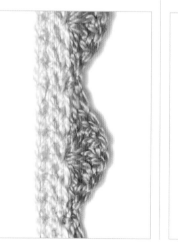

2   SCALLOP EDGE
Directory view, page 10

Skill level: Beginner/easy

Cotton perle

METHOD

Make a foundation chain of the required length, or work row 1 directly into the item to be trimmed with right side facing. (multiple of 3 stitches + 1)
Row 1: 3 ch, 1 dc in each st to end, turn.
Row 2: 1 ch, *2 ch, skip 2 sts, 1 sc in next st, rep from * to end, turn.
Row 3: 1ch, *(1 sc, 1 hdc, 1 dc, 1 tr, 1 dc, 1 hdc, 1 sc) in 2-ch sp, rep from * to end. Fasten off.

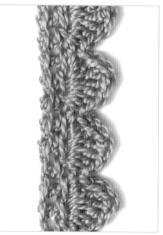

3   GLITZY EDGE
Directory view, page 10

Skill level: Beginner/easy

 Cotton perle

25 mm circular holographic sequins

METHOD

Thread the sequins onto the yarn before beginning.
Make a foundation chain of the required length, or work row 1 directly into the item to be trimmed with right side facing. (multiple of 4 stitches + 1)
Row 1: 1 ch, 1 sc in each st to end, turn.
Row 2: As row 1.
Row 3: 3 ch, 1 dc in each st to end, turn.
Row 4: 3 ch, *3 dc, pull down first sequin into next dc, rep from * to end. Fasten off.

4   LARGE PICOT EDGE
Directory view, page 11

Skill level: Beginner/easy

Cotton perle

METHOD

Make a foundation chain of the required length, or work row 1 directly into the item to be trimmed with right side facing. (multiple of 3 stitches + 1)
Row 1: 1 ch, 1 sc in each st to end, turn.
Row 2: As row 1.
Row 3: 1 ch, *1 sc, 5 ch, 1 ss in first of these 5 ch, skip 1 st, 1 sc, rep from * to end. Fasten off.

5   BLOCK EDGE
Directory view, page 11

Skill level: Intermediate

Cotton perle

METHOD

Make a foundation chain of the required length, or work row 1 directly into the item to be trimmed with right side facing. (multiple of 4 stitches + 1)
Row 1: 1 ch, 1 sc in each st to end, turn.
Row 2: As row 1.
Row 3: 4 ch, *skip 3 sts, 1 tr in next st, 3 ch, 4 dc around stem of tr just worked, rep from * to end. Fasten off.

6   SHELLS AND BEADS
Directory view, page 11

Skill level: Intermediate

DK (double knitting)

5 mm glass seed beads

METHOD

Thread the beads onto the yarn before beginning.
Make a foundation chain of the required length, or work row 1 directly into the item to be trimmed with right side facing. (multiple of 6 stitches + 1)
Row 1: 1 ch, 1 sc in 2nd ch from hook, *3 ch, skip 3 sts, 3 sc, rep from * to end, turn.
Row 2: 1 ch, 1sc, skip 1 st *(5 dc in 3-ch sp—working bead into 3rd of these dc), skip 1 st, 1 sc in next st, skip 1 st, rep from * to end. Fasten off.

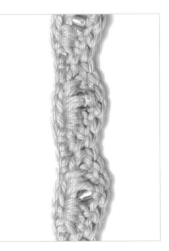

REGULAR WAVES
Directory view, page 11

Skill level: Beginner/easy

 *Cotton perle*

METHOD

Make a foundation chain of the required length, or work row 1 directly into the item to be trimmed with right side facing. (multiple of 10 stitches + 1)
Row 1: 1 ch, 1 sc in 2nd ch from hook, *5 dc, 5 sc, rep from * to end, turn.
Row 2: 1 ch, 4 sc, 5 dc, * 5 sc, 5 dc, rep from * to last st, 1 sc. Fasten off.

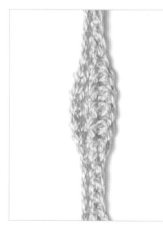

---

8 FUZZY EDGE
Directory view, page 11

Skill level: Beginner/easy

Worked in two yarns: cotton perle (smooth) and DK eyelash yarn (fuzzy)

METHOD

Using the smooth yarn, make a foundation chain of the required length, or work row 1 directly into the item to be trimmed with right side facing.
(any number of stitches)
Row 1: (smooth) 1 ch, 1 sc in each chain to end, turn.
Row 2: (smooth) 3 ch, 1 dc in each st to end. Fasten off.
Row 3: (fuzzy) As row 1.
Row 4: (fuzzy) As row 1. Fasten off.

---

9 ARCADE EDGE
Directory view, page 11

Skill level: Beginner/easy

Cotton perle

METHOD

Make a foundation chain of the required length, or work row 1 directly into the item to be trimmed with right side facing. (multiple of 6 stitches + 3)
Row 1: 1 ch, 1 sc in each st to end, turn.
Row 2: 1 ch, 2 sc, *3 ch, skip 3 sts, 3 sc, rep from * to end, turn.
Row 3: 1 ch, 1 sc, *5 dc in 3-ch sp, skip 1 st, 1 sc, skip 1 st, rep from * to end. Fasten off.

 **SHARP CHEVRONS**
Directory view, page 12

Skill level: Intermediate

Cotton perle

METHOD

Make a foundation chain of the required length, or work row 1 directly into the item to be trimmed with right side facing. (multiple of 16 stitches)
Row 1: 3 ch, 1 dc in 4th ch from hook, *4 dc, (dc3tog) twice, 4 dc, (3 dc in next st) twice, rep from * to end, omitting last 3 dc of final repeat. Fasten off.

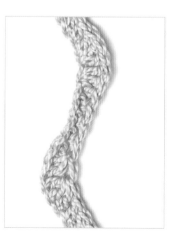

LATTICE CHEVRONS
Directory view, page 12

Skill level: Intermediate

 *Cotton perle*

METHOD

Make a foundation chain of the required length, or work row 1 directly into the item to be trimmed with right side facing. (multiple of 20 stitches + 1)
Row 1: 4 ch, 1 dc in 5th ch from hook, *(1 ch, skip 1 st, 1 dc) 3 times, 1 ch, skip 1 st, (dc 2 tog) working 1st dc in next st, skip 3 ch and 2nd dc in next st), (1 ch, skip 1 st, 1 dc in next st) 3 times, 1 ch, skip 1 st, (1 dc, 3 ch, 1 dc in next st), rep from * to end, turn.
Row 2: 6 ch, 1 dc in 3-ch loop, *6 dc, (dc2tog) working 1st dc in next st, skip 3 st and 2nd dc in next st), 6 dc, (1 dc, 3 ch, 1 dc) in 3-ch sp, rep from * to end. Fasten off.

SOFT EDGE
Directory view, page 12

Skill level: Beginner/easy

 *Worked in two yarns: cotton perle (smooth) and mohair*

METHOD

Using the smooth yarn, make a foundation chain of the required length, or work row 1 directly into the item to be trimmed with right side facing.
(odd number of stitches)
Row 1: (smooth) 1 ch, 1 sc in each st to end. Fasten off, turn.
Row 2: (mohair) 3 ch, 1 dc in same st, *skip 1 st, 2 dc in next st, rep from * to end. Fasten off.

ARCHES EDGE
Directory view, page 12

Skill level: Beginner/easy

 *Variegated cotton perle*

METHOD

Make a foundation chain of the required length, or work row 1 directly into the item to be trimmed with right side facing. (multiple of 5 stitches + 3)
Row 1: 1 ch, 1 sc in each st to end, turn.
Row 2: 1 ch, *2 sc, 5 ch, skip 2 sts, 3 sc, rep from * to end, turn.
Row 3: As row 1. Fasten off.

PICOT ARCHES
Directory view, page 12

Skill level: Intermediate

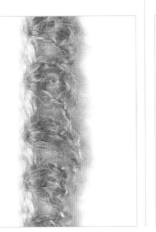 *Cotton perle*

METHOD

Notes: picot = 3 ch, sl st into 3rd ch from hook.
Make a foundation chain of the required length, or work row 1 directly into the item to be trimmed with right side facing. (multiple of 6 stitches)
Row 1: 1 ch, 1 sc in each st to end, turn.
Row 2: 1 ch, 1 sc in first st, *5 ch, skip 4 sts, 1 sc in next st, 3 picots, 1 sc in next st, rep from * to last 5 sts, 5 ch, skip 4 sts, 1 sc in last st, turn.
Row 3: 3 ch, 1 sc in 5-ch arch, *8ch, 1 sc in 5-ch arch, rep from * to last 5-ch arch, 2 ch, 1 sc in last st, turn.
Row 4: 1 ch, skip 2-ch arch, 1 sc in next sc, *11 sc in 8-ch arch, 1 sc in next st, rep from * to end. Fasten off.

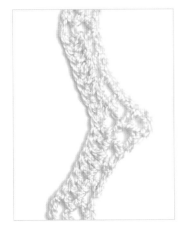

15 RHYTHMIC EDGE

Directory view, page 13

Skill level: Beginner/easy

 *Cotton perle*

METHOD

Make a foundation chain of the required length, or work row 1 directly into the item to be trimmed with right side facing. (multiple of 8 stitches + 1)
Row 1: 1 ch, 1 sc in each st to end, turn.
Row 2: As row 1.
Row 3: 1 ch, *6 sc, skip 2 sc, 6 dc, rep from * to end, turn.
Row 4: As row 1. Fasten off.

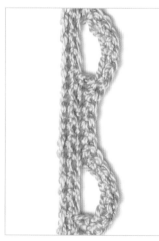

16 BEADED WAVES

Directory view, page 13

Skill level: Intermediate

 *Cotton perle*

3 mm glass seed beads

METHOD

Thread the beads onto the yarn before beginning.
Make a foundation chain of the required length, or work row 1 directly into the item to be trimmed with right side facing. (odd number of stitches)
Row 1: 1 ch, 1 sc in each st to end, turn.
Row 2: 3 ch, *bring down a bead to work into next dc, 1 dc, rep from * to end
Row 3: 1 ch, *1 hdc, 1 sc, rep from * to end. Fasten off.

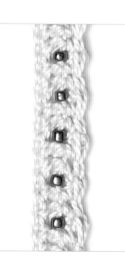

17 SCALLOPED ARCHES

Directory view, page 13

Skill level: Beginner/easy

 *Cotton perle*

METHOD

Make a foundation chain of the required length, or work row 1 directly into the item to be trimmed with right side facing. (multiple of 4 stitches + 1)
Row 1: 1 ch, 1 sc in each st to end, turn.
Row 2: 1 ch, *5 ch, skip 3 sts, 1 sc into next st, rep * to end, turn.
Row 3: 1 ch, *7 ch, skip 5-ch loop, 1 sc into next st, rep from * to end. Fasten off.

18 ARCH AND PICOT EDGE

Directory view, page 13

Skill level: Intermediate

Cotton perle

METHOD

Make a foundation chain of the required length, or work row 1 directly into the item to be trimmed with right side facing. (multiple of 5 stitches + 1)
Row 1: 1 ch, 1 sc in each st to end, turn.
Row 2: 1 ch, *5 ch, sl st into 3rd ch from hook, 3 ch, skip 4 sts, 1 sc in next st, rep from * to end, turn.
Row 3: 1 ch, *6 ch, sl st into 3rd ch from hook, 4 ch, skip 4 sts, 1 sc in next st, rep from * to end. Fasten off.

SHALLOW SCALLOPS

Directory view, page 13

Skill level: Intermediate

 *Worked in cotton perle in two colors: A and B*

METHOD

Using color A, make a foundation chain of the required length, or work row I directly into the item to be trimmed with right side facing. (multiple of 6 stitches + 2)

Row I: (A) I ch, I sc in each st to end, turn.

Row 2: (A) 3 ch, I dc, *I ch, skip I st, 2 dc, rep from * to end. Fasten off, turn.

Row 3: (B) *4 ch, I sc in next ch sp, rep from * to last ch sp, 2 ch, I sc in last st, turn.

Row 4: (B) I ch, I sc in 2-ch sp, *5 dc in next 4-ch sp, I sc in next 4-ch sp, rep from * to end. Fasten off.

MESH ARCHES

Directory view, page 14

Skill level: Beginner/easy

Cotton perle

METHOD

Make a foundation chain of the required length, or work row I directly into the item to be trimmed with right side facing. (multiple of 4 stitches + I)

Row I: 4 ch, I dc in 7th ch from hook, *I ch, skip I st, I dc in next st, rep from * to end, turn.

Row 2: I ch, *5 ch, (skip I ch, I dc, I ch), I sc in next st, rep from * to end, turn.

Row 3: I ch, *7 sc in 5-ch arch, I sc in next st, rep from * to end. Fasten off.

IRIS EDGE

Directory view, page 14

Skill level: Intermediate

Cotton perle

METHOD

Make a foundation chain of the required length, or work row I directly into the item to be trimmed with right side facing. (multiple of 4 stitches + I)

Row I: 3 ch, (I dc, I ch, 2 dc) in 4th ch from hook, *skip 3 ch, (2 dc, I ch, 2 dc) in next st, rep from * to end. Fasten off.

BEADS AND DOUBLES

Directory view, page 14

Skill level: Intermediate

Cotton perle

5 mm glass seed beads

METHOD

Thread the beads onto the yarn before beginning.

Make a foundation chain of the required length, or work row I directly into the item to be trimmed with right side facing. (multiple of 4 stitches + 3)

Row I: I ch, I sc in each st to end, turn.

Row 2: 3 ch, 2 dc, *skip I sc, bring down bead work into next sc, 2 dc, rep from * to end, turn.

Row 3: As row I. Fasten off.

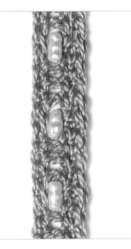

23 CHAIN ARCHES

Directory view, page 14

Skill level: Beginner/easy

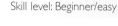 *Cotton perle*

METHOD

Make a foundation chain of the required length, or work row 1 directly into the item to be trimmed with right side facing. (odd number of stitches)

Row 1: 1 ch, 1 sc in each st to end, turn.

Row 2: As row 1.

Row 3: 1 ch, *3 ch, skip 1 st, 1 sc in next st, rep from * to end. Fasten off.

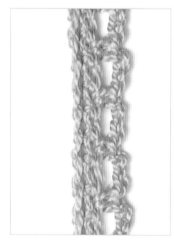

24 WAVES EDGE

Directory view, page 14

Skill level: Intermediate

 Cotton perle

METHOD

Make a foundation chain of the required length, or work row 1 directly into the item to be trimmed with right side facing. (multiple of 6 stitches + 3)

Row 1: 1 ch, 1 sc in each st to end, turn.

Row 2: As row 1.

Row 3: As row 1.

Row 4: 1 ch, 2 sc, *6 ch, skip 3 sts, 3 sc, rep from * to end, turn.

Row 5: 1 ch, 2 sc, *(3 sc, 1 hdc, 1 dc, 1 hdc, 3 sc) in 6-ch loop, 3 sc, rep from * to end. Fasten off.

25 LAYERED CHAINS

Directory view, page 15

Skill level: Intermediate

 *Worked in cotton perle in three colors: A, B, and C*

METHOD

Using color A, make a foundation chain of the required length, or work row 1 directly into the item to be trimmed with right side facing. (multiple of 3 stitches + 1)

Row 1: (A) 1 ch, 1 sc in each st to end, turn.

Row 2: (A) As row 1.

Row 3: (A) As row 1. Fasten off, turn.

Row 4: (B) 3 ch, 1 dc in first st, *5 ch, skip 2 sts, 1 dc in next st, rep from * to end. Fasten off, turn.

Row 5: Join in color C to left of 1st dc in row 1 and work as row 4. Fasten off.

26 SIMPLY BEADS

Directory view, page 15

Skill level: Intermediate

 *Cotton perle*

3 mm glass seed beads

METHOD

Thread the beads onto the yarn before beginning.

Make a foundation chain of the required length, or work row 1 directly into the item to be trimmed with right side facing. (multiple of 10 stitches + 1)

Row 1: 1 ch, 1 sc in each st to end, turn.

Row 2: 3 ch, *1 dc, bring down bead in next dc, rep from * to end, turn.

Row 3: As row 2.

Row 4: As row 1.

Row 5: 1 ch, *bring down bead in next sc, 4 sc, rep from * to end. Fasten off.

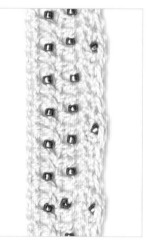

27 FLORAL EDGE
Directory view, page 15

Skill level: Intermediate

 *Cotton perle*

METHOD

Make a foundation chain of the required length, or work row 1 directly into the item to be trimmed with right side facing. (multiple of 4 stitches + 1)
Row 1: 3 ch, (1 dc, 1 ch, 2 dc) in same st, *skip 3 ch, (2 dc, 1 ch, 2 dc) in next st, rep from * to end, turn.
Row 2: 3 ch, (1 dc, 1 ch, 2 dc) in first ch sp, (2 dc, 1 ch, 2 dc) in each ch sp to end. Fasten off.

---

28 POSY EDGE
Directory view, page 15

Skill level: Intermediate

Cotton perle

METHOD

There is no foundation chain for this edging.
Row 1: 4 ch, 1 dc in 4th ch from hook (center ring made), (3 ch, 2 dc into ring, 3 ch, 1 sl st in ring) 3 times (3 petals made = 1 motif), *11 ch, 1 dc into 4th ch from hook, 3 ch, 1 dc in ring, 1 sl st between 2 dc of last petal made, 1 dc into ring, 3 ch, 1 sl st in ring, (3 ch, 2 dc in ring, 3 ch, 1 sl st in ring) twice, rep from * to length required. Fasten off.

---

29 IRIS STITCH EDGE
Directory view, page 15

Skill level: Challenging/complex

Cotton perle

METHOD

Make a foundation chain of the required length, or work row 1 directly into the item to be trimmed with right side facing. (multiple of 4 stitches + 1)
Row 1: 4 ch, 3 dc in 5th ch from hook, *skip 3 ch, (1 dc, 3 ch, 3 dc) in next st, rep from * to end. Fasten off.

---

30 UNDULATING EDGE
Directory view, page 16

Skill level: Intermediate

Cotton perle

METHOD

Notes: Picot = 3 ch, sl st into 3rd ch from hook.
Make a foundation chain of the required length, or work row 1 directly into the item to be trimmed with right side facing. (multiple of 12 + 3 stitches)
Row 1: 1 ch, 1 sc in each st or position to end, turn.
Row 2: 1 ch, 2 sc, *2 hdc, 2 dc, 2 tr, 2 dc, 2 hdc, 2 dc, rep from * to end, turn.
Row 3: 1 ch, *1 sc in each of next 6 sts, picot between 2 tr, 1 sc in each of next 6 sts, rep from * to last 2 sts, 2 sc. Fasten off.

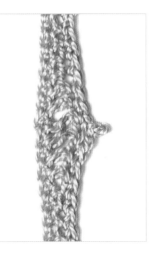

31 INTERLACED EDGE

Directory view, page 16

Skill level: Intermediate

 Cotton perle

METHOD

Make a foundation chain of the required length, or work row 1 directly into the item to be trimmed with right side facing. (multiple of 16 stitches + 1)
Row 1: 1 ch, 2 sc in 2nd ch from hook, *1 sc in each of next 7 ch, skip 1 ch, 1 sc in each of next 7 ch, 3 sc in next ch, rep from * to end, omitting 1 dc at end of last rep, turn.
Row 2: 1 ch, 2 sc in first sc, *1 sc in each of next 7 sc, skip 2 sc, 1 sc in each of next 7 sc, 3 sc in next sc, rep from * to end omitting 1 dc at end of last rep. Rep row 2 for required length. Fasten off.

32 DEEP RIPPLES

Directory view, page 16

Skill level: Beginner/easy

 Cotton perle

METHOD

Make a foundation chain of the required length, or work row 1 directly into the item to be trimmed with right side facing. (any number of stitches)
Row 1: 1 ch, 1 sc in each st to end, turn.
Row 2: As row 1.
Row 3: As row 1.
Row 4: 1 ch, 1 sc in first st, 5 ch, *(1 sc, 5 ch) in next st, rep from * to end, omitting last 5 ch. Fasten off.

33 SHALLOW RIPPLES

Directory view, page 16

Skill level: Beginner/easy

 Cotton perle

METHOD

Make a foundation chain of the required length, or work row 1 directly into the item to be trimmed with right side facing. (even number of stitches)
Row 1: 1 ch, 1 sc in each ch or position to end, turn.
Row 2: 1 ch, *1 sc, 2 ch, skip 1 ch, rep from * to end, omitting last 2 ch, turn.
Row 3: 1 ch, *(1 sc, 1 ch, 1 hdc, 1 ch, 1 dc, 1 ch, 1 hdc, 1 ch, 1 sc) in 2-ch loop, rep from * to end. Fasten off.

34 FRILLY EDGE

Directory view, page 17

Skill level: Beginner/easy

 Cotton perle

METHOD

Make a foundation chain of the required length, or work row 1 directly into the item to be trimmed with right side facing. (any number of stitches)
Row 1: 1 ch, 1 sc in each ch to end, turn.
Row 2: As row 1.
Row 3: 3 ch, 1 dc in each sc to end, turn.
Row 4: 2 ch, (3 dc, 1 ch) in each dc to end. Omit 1 ch at end of row. Fasten off.

35 ## SURFACE BLOCKS
Directory view, page 17

Skill level: Beginner/easy

 *Worked in cotton perle in two colors: A and B*

METHOD

Make a foundation chain of the required length, or work row 1 directly into the item to be trimmed with right side facing. (multiple of 7 stitches + 1)
Row 1: 3 ch, 1 dc in 4th ch from hook, 1 dc in each ch to end, turn.
Rows 2–6: 1 ch, 1 sc into each st to end, turn. Fasten off.
Raised stitch: Using a contrasting color yarn, starting at the dc row, holding the crochet hook on top of the work with the incoming yarn held in the normal way, under the fabric, work *4 ch across middle of dc row, 2 ch down, 4 ch across, 2 ch up, rep from * to end. Fasten off.

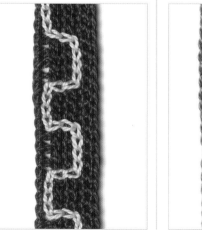

36 ## PARALLEL LINES
Directory view, page 17

Skill level: Beginner/easy

Worked in cotton perle in three colors

METHOD

Make a foundation chain of the required length, or work row 1 directly into the item to be trimmed with right side facing. (any number of stitches)
Row 1: 3 ch, 1 dc in 4th ch from hook, 1 dc in each ch to end, turn.
Rows 2–5: 1 ch, 1 sc into each st to end, turn.
Row 6: 3 ch, 1 dc in 4th ch from hook, 1 dc in each ch to end, turn.
Fasten off.
Raised stitch: Using a contrasting color yarn, starting at the top edge, holding the crochet hook on top of the work with the incoming yarn held in the normal way, but under the edging, make a sl st onto hook, work a straight line to end.
Using a second contrasting yarn, working in the same way, sl st another line next to the first, fasten off.

37 ## FRILLED EDGING
Directory view, page 17

Skill level: Intermediate

Cotton perle

METHOD

Make a foundation chain of the required length, or work row 1 directly into the item to be trimmed with right side facing. (even number of stitches)
Row 1: 1 ch, 1 sc in each ch to end, turn.
Row 2: *5 ch, skip next st, sl st into next st, rep from * to end, turn.
Row 3: 1 ch, (1 sc, [3 ch, 1 sc] 5 times) in each 1-ch sp to end. Fasten off.

FRINGES

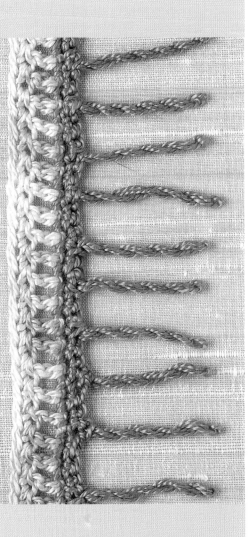

SEE ALSO

*Standard crochet abbreviations, page 125
Refresher course, pages 110–125*

 38 **BEADED FILET FRINGE**
Directory view, page 18

Skill level: Beginner/easy

 Double knitting (DK weight)

5 mm glass seed beads

METHOD

Make a foundation chain of the required length, or work row 1 directly into the item to be trimmed with right side facing. (multiple of 4 stitches + 1)
Row 1: 5 ch, 1 dc in 10th ch from hook, *3 ch, skip 3 sts, 1 dc in next st, rep from * to end, turn.
Row 2: 1 ch, *2 ch, 1 sc in 3 ch space, 2 ch, 1 dc in next dc, rep from * to end. Fasten off.
Fringe: Basic fringe pattern, threading a bead over the loop (double thickness of yarn), attach as described on page 119, to dcs on last row to end. Fasten off.

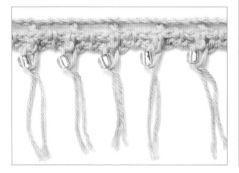

39 **TRIPLE LOOP FRINGE**
Directory view, page 18

Skill level: Intermediate

Double knitting (DK weight)

METHOD

Make a foundation chain of the required length, or work row 1 directly into the item to be trimmed with right side facing. (multiple of 4 stitches + 1)
Row 1: 1 ch, 1 sc in each ch to end, turn.
Row 2: 1 ch, *5 ch, skip 3 sts, 1 dc in back loop only of next st, rep from * to end, turn.
Row 3: 3 ch, *1 sc, 5 ch, 1 sc in 5-ch loop, rep from * to last loop, 2 ch, 1 sc in last st, turn.
Row 4: 2 ch, 1 sc in 2-ch loop, *2 ch, 1 sc in 5-ch loop, 2 ch, skip 1 sc, 1 sc in next sc, rep from * to last loop, 2 ch, 1 sc in last st. Fasten off.
Fringe: Make a basic fringe using three lengths of yarn in each 2-chain space, giving a delicate style.

40 **BLOCK FRINGE**
Directory view, page 19

Skill level: Intermediate

 Worked in cotton perle in two colors

METHOD

Make a foundation chain of the required length, or work row 1 directly into the item to be trimmed with right side facing.
(multiple of 8 stitches + 1)
Row 1: 1 ch, 1 sc in each st to end, turn.
Row 2: As row 1.
Row 3: 3 ch, *1 dc in each st to end, turn.
Row 4: As row 3.
Row 5: As row 3.
Row 6: As row 1. Fasten off.
Fringe: Fold two lengths of a contrasting yarn and knot around a dc on row 2, add another three fringes in the same way, skip the next 4 dc, repeat this pattern across the row. You could also work fringes on 2, 3, or 4 consecutive rows for a denser look.

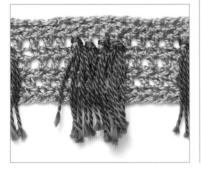

41 **OPEN BLOCK FRINGE**
Directory view, page 19

Skill level: Beginner/easy

 *Worked in double knitting (DK weight) in two colors*

METHOD

Make a foundation chain of the required length, or work row 1 directly into the item to be trimmed with right side facing.
(multiple of 6 stitches + 1)
Row 1: 1 ch, 1 sc in each chain to end, turn.
Row 2: 3 ch, *3 ch, skip 3 sts, 3 dc, rep from * to end. Fasten off.
Fringe: Using a single strand of contrasting yarn, *knot one piece in the first 3-chain space, two separate lengths in the next 3-chain space, repeat from * to end.

42 **RANDOM FRINGE**
Directory view, page 19

Skill level: Intermediate

Worked in cotton perle in two colors

METHOD

Notes: Loop st: the loops will appear on the wrong side of the fabric as the loops are formed at the back of the fabric. Work the loop stitch as follows:
1. Insert hook into the st below, as usual. Using a finger of the free hand, pull up the yarn to form a loop of the required size. Pick up both strands of the loop and draw them through.
2. Wrap the yarn over the hook.
3. Draw the yarn through all 3 loops.
If the fringe loops hang the wrong way, straighten them by pinning and steaming in place.

Make a foundation chain of the required length, or work row 1 directly into the item to be trimmed with right side facing. (multiple of 8 stitches + 1) (To ensure that this fringe is on the correct side for your project, repeat row 1 if necessary.)
Row 1: 1 ch, 1 sc in each chain to end, turn.
Rows 2–3: As row 1.
Row 4: 1 ch, *1 loop st in each of next 4 sts, 1 sc in each of next 4 sts, rep from * to end, turn.
Row 5: As row 1. Fasten off.
.

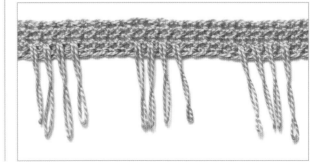

43 ### SINGLE CROCHET FRINGE
Directory view, page 19

Skill level: Beginner/easy

 Cotton perle

METHOD

Make a foundation chain of the required length, or work row I directly into the item to be trimmed with right side facing.
(multiple of 3 stitches + I)
Row I: I ch, I sc in each chain to end, turn.
Row 2: I ch, *2 sc, 8 ch for fringe, I sc in 2nd ch from hook, 6 sc into fringe ch, I sl st in last sc worked on heading of fringe, I sc. Fasten off.

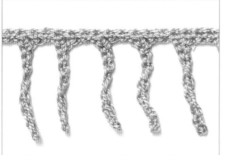

44 ### TWISTED FRINGE
Directory view, page 20

Skill level: Challenging/complex

 Worked in cotton perle in two colors: multicolored yarn and plain yarn

METHOD

Using the multicolored yarn make a foundation chain of the required length or work row I directly into the item to be trimmed with right side facing.
(multiple of 3 stitches + I)
Row I: (multicolored yarn) I ch, I sc in each chain to end. Fasten off, turn.
Row 2: (multicolored yarn) 3 ch, I dc in each sc to end, turn.
Row 3: (plain yarn) As row I.
Row 4: (plain yarn) I ch, *2 sc, (I sc in next st, extend loop on hook to twice the required fringe length, with hook still in the loop twist 8 times, allow the loop to twist tog, I sc into same stitch), rep from * to last st, I sc, rep from * to end. Fasten off.

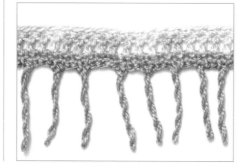

45 ### CURLICUE FRINGE
Directory view, page 20

Skill level: Challenging/complex

 Worked in cotton perle in two colors: A and B

METHOD

Using yarn A, make a foundation chain of the required length, or work row I directly into the item to be trimmed with right side facing.
(multiple of 4 stitches + I)
Row I: (A) I ch, I sc in each chain to end, turn.
Row 2: (A) 2 ch, I hdc in each st to end, turn.
Row 3: (A) As row 2. Fasten off, turn.
Row 4: (B) I ch, *3 sc, ^9 ch, 4 sc in 3rd ch from hook, (4 dc in next ch) 6 times, I sl st in last sc worked on fringe header ^, rep from ^ to ^ once, rep from * to end. Fasten off.

46 CORKSCREW FRINGE
Directory view, page 20

Skill level: Challenging/complex

 Cotton perle

METHOD

Make a foundation chain of the required length, or work row 1 directly into the item to be trimmed with right side facing.
(multiple of 3 stitches + 1)
Row 1: 1 ch, 1 sc in each chain to end, turn.
Row 2: As row 1.
Row 3: 1 ch, *3 sc, 9 ch, 4 sc in 2nd ch from hook, (4 sc in next st) 7 times, 1 sl st in last sc worked on fringe header, rep from * to end. Fasten off.

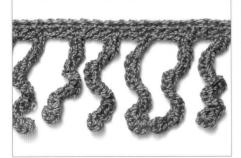

47 SUPER SEQUINS
Directory view, page 20

Skill level: Beginner/easy

 Cotton perle

20 mm sequins in a range of colors

METHOD

Thread the sequins onto the yarn before starting work.
Make a foundation chain of the required length, or work row 1 directly into the item to be trimmed with right side facing.
(multiple of 6 stitches + 1)
Row 1: 1 ch, 1 sc in each chain to end, turn.
Row 2: 3 ch, *5 ch, bring down 1 sequin to be worked in next st, 1 sc in 2nd ch from hook, 1 sc in each of next 3 ch, 1 sl st in top of st on main section of fringe, 1 dc in each of next 5 sc, rep from * to end. Fasten off.

48 RINGLET FRINGE
Directory view, page 21

Skill level: Challenging/complex

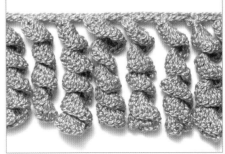 *Cotton perle*

METHOD

Make a foundation chain of the required length, or work row 1 directly into the item to be trimmed with right side facing.
(multiple of 3 stitches + 1)
Row 1: 1 ch, 1 sc in each chain to end, turn.
Row 2: 1 ch, *3 sc, 9 ch, 6 dc in 4th chain from hook, (6 dc in next st) 5 times, 1 sl st in last sc worked on fringe header, rep from * to end. Fasten off.

49 **SLIP FRINGE**
Directory view, page 21

Skill level: Beginner/easy

 Cotton perle

METHOD

Make a foundation chain of the required length, or work row 1 directly into the item to be trimmed with right side facing.
(multiple of 3 stitches + 1)
Row 1: 1 ch, 1 sc in each chain to end, turn.
Row 2: 3 ch, 1 dc in each st to end, turn.
Row 3: 1 ch, *2 sc, 9 ch, 1 sl st in 2nd ch from hook, 1 sl st in each of next 7 ch, 1 sl st in last sc worked on fringe header, 1 sc, rep from * to end. Fasten off.

 50 **TWISTED BULLIONS**
Directory view, page 21

Skill level: Complex/challenging

 Cotton perle

METHOD

Notes: Bullion stitch = yo 5 times, insert hook in next stitch and draw through a loop, yo and draw through all loops on hook, 1 chain.
Make a foundation chain of the required length, or work row 1 directly into the item to be trimmed with right side facing.
(multiple of 6 stitches + 1)
Row 1: 1 ch, 1 sc in each chain to end, turn.
Row 2: As row 1.
Row 3: As row 1.
Row 4: As row 1.
Row 5: 1 ch, *5 sc, 5 ch, 4 bullion sts in 2nd ch from hook, 3 sl st in fringe chain, 1 sl st in last sc worked on fringe header, 1 sc, rep from * to last st, 1 sc. Fasten off.

 51 **ONLY BEADS**
Directory view, page 21

Skill level: Intermediate

 Cotton perle

 3 mm glass seed beads

METHOD

Thread the beads onto the yarn before starting work, allowing 12 beads per loop. Make a foundation chain of the required length, or work row 1 directly into the item to be trimmed with right side facing.
(multiple of 3 stitches + 1)
Row 1: 1 ch, 1 sc in each chain to end, turn.
Row 2: As row 1.
Row 3: As row 1.
Row 4: 1 ch, *2 sc, bring down 12 beads and sc in next st (loop formed), rep from * to end. Fasten off.

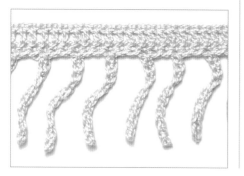

52 LATTICE FRINGE
Directory view, page 22

Skill level: Beginner/easy

 Cotton perle

METHOD

Make a foundation chain of the required length, or work row I directly into the item to be trimmed with right side facing. (multiple of 6 stitches + 3)
Row I: I ch, I sc in each chain to end, turn.
Row 2: 3 ch, 2 dc, *3 ch, skip 3 sts, 3 dc, rep from * to end, turn.
Row 3: As row I. Fasten off.
Fringe: Using a single length of yarn, make two knots around row 3 in each 3-ch space.

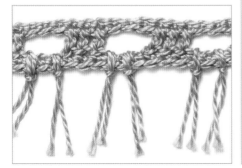

53 PARTLY BEADS
Directory view, page 22

Skill level: Beginner/easy

 Cotton perle

 3 mm glass seed beads

METHOD

Make a foundation chain of the required length, or work row I directly into the item to be trimmed with right side facing. (multiple of 3 stitches + I)
Thread the beads onto the yarn before starting work, allowing 8 beads per loop.
Row I: I ch, I sc in each chain to end, turn.
Row 2: As row I.
Row 3: As row I.
Row 4: I ch, *2 sc, bring down 8 beads, sc in next st, rep from * to end, turn.
Row 5: As row I. Fasten off.

54 UNDULATING FRINGE
Directory view, page 22

Skill level: Complex challenging

 Cotton perle

METHOD

Make a foundation chain of the required length, or work row I directly into the item to be trimmed with right side facing. (multiple of 3 stitches + I)
Row I: I ch, I sc in each chain to end, turn.
Row 2: As row I.
Row 3: I ch, *2 sc, II ch, I sc in 2nd ch from hook, I hdc, I dc, I hdc, 2 sc, I hdc, I sc, I sl st in last sc worked on fringe header, I sc, rep from * to last st, I sc. Fasten off.

55 EYELASH FRINGE

Directory view, page 22

Skill level: Beginner/easy

 Worked in two yarns: cotton perle and eyelash yarn

METHOD

Make a foundation chain of the required length, or work row 1 directly into the item to be trimmed with right side facing. (any number of stitches)
Row 1: 1 ch, 1 sc in each chain to end, turn.
Row 2: 3 ch, 1 dc in each st to end, turn.
Row 3: As row 1. Fasten off.
Fringe: Knot one length of eyelash yarn around stem of each sc on row 3.

56 POPCORN FRINGE

Directory view, page 23

Skill level: Intermediate

 Double knitting (DK weight)

METHOD

Notes: Popcorn = work 5 dc in same st, slip last loop off hook, insert hook in top loop of first treble, reinsert in top loop of last dc, pull this loop through to close the top of popcorn st.
Make a foundation chain of the required length, or work row 1 directly into the item to be trimmed with right side facing.
(multiple of 5 stitches + 4)
Row 1: 1 ch, 1 sc in each chain to end, turn.
Row 2: 1 ch, 3 sc in front loop only, *popcorn, 4 sc in front loop only, rep from * to end, turn.
Row 3: 1 ch, 1 sc in front loop of each st to end, turn.
Row 4: As row 1. Fasten off.
Fringe: Knot three lengths of yarn into row 4, in line with the popcorn.

57 BEADED TRIANGLES

Directory view, page 23

Skill level: Intermediate

 Cotton perle

5 mm glass seed beads

METHOD

Thread the beads onto the yarn before starting work.
Make a foundation chain of the required length, or work row 1 directly into the item to be trimmed with right side facing.
(multiple of 8 stitches + 1)
Row 1: 1 ch, 1 sc in each ch to end, turn.
Row 2: 3 ch, 1 dc, *bring down a bead, 2 dc, rep from * to end, omitting bead on last rep, turn.
Row 3: As row 2.
Row 4: 1 ch, 1 sc in each st, turn.
Row 5: 1 ch, 1 sc in first st *6 ch, bring down and enclose a bead in 1 sc in 2nd ch from hook, 1 hdc, 1 dc, 1 tr, 1 dtr, skip 5 sc, 1 sc in each of next 3 sc, rep from * to end. Fasten off.
Fringe: Make a basic fringe (see page 119) using two lengths of yarn, placing them at the point with the bead.

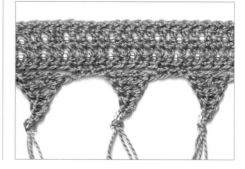

58 BEADED LOOPS
Directory view, page 23

Skill level: Intermediate

 Cotton perle

 3 mm glass seed beads

METHOD

Make a foundation chain of the required length, or work row 1 directly into the item to be trimmed with right side facing. (multiple of 4 stitches + 1)
Row 1: 1 ch, 1 sc in each ch to end, turn.
Row 2: 2 ch, *bring down a bead, 2 dc, rep from * to end, omitting bead on last rep, turn.
Row 3: As row 2.
Row 4: 1 ch, *3 sc, bring down 10 beads, 1 sc in next st to complete the fringe loop, rep from * to end. Fasten off.

---

59 CHEVRON FRINGE
Directory view, page 24

Skill level: Challenging/complex

 *Cotton perle*

METHOD

Make a foundation chain of the required length, or work row 1 directly into the item to be trimmed with right side facing. (multiple of 16 stitches + 2)
Row 1: 2 sc in 2nd ch from hook, *1 sc in each of next 7 ch, skip 1 ch, 1 sc in each of next 7 ch, 3 sc in next ch, rep from * to end, omitting 1 sc at end of last rep, turn.
Row 2: 1 ch, 1 sc in first sc, *1 sc in each of next 7 sc, skip 2 sc, 1 sc in next 7 sc, 3 sc into next sc, rep from * to end omitting 1 sc at end of last rep.
Row 3–5: As row 2. Fasten off.
Fringe: Using the same color of yarn, with right side and cast-off edge closest. The idea of this fringe is that there are two levels of fringe facing downward toward row 5. Using the basic fringe method (see page 119), attach 3 yarn lengths to the lower level or cast-off edge. Upper level is worked on the second row from cast-on or fabric edge, allowing space to attach to an item.

---

60 BEADED CHEVRONS FRINGE
Directory view, page 24

Skill level: Intermediate

 *Worked in fingering weight wool mixture yarn and cotton perle*

3 mm glass seed beads

METHOD

Make a foundation chain of the required length, or work row 1 directly into the item to be trimmed with right side facing. (multiple of 16 stitches + 2)
Row 1: 2 sc in 2nd ch from hook, *1 sc in each of next 7 ch, skip 1 ch, 1 sc in each of next 7 ch, 3 sc into next ch, rep from * to end, omitting 1 sc at end of last rep, turn.
Row 2: 1 ch, 1 sc into first sc, *1 sc into each of next 7 sc, skip 2 sc, 1 sc into next 7 sc, 3 sc into next sc, rep from * to end omitting 1 sc at end of last rep.
Row 3–4: As row 2. Fasten off.
Fringe: Using the basic fringe method (see page 119), thread 2 beads onto 2 lengths of contrasting color yarn. Keeping the beads in the center, attach to the points of the chevrons.

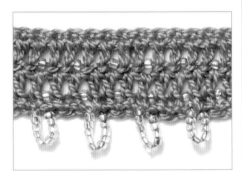

61 PEARL LEAF FRINGE
Directory view, page 25

Skill level: Challenging/complex

 *Cotton perle*

10 mm pearl leaf beads

METHOD

Notes: Thread the beads onto the yarn before starting work.
Make a foundation chain of the required length, or work row I directly into the item to be trimmed with right side facing.
(multiple of 5 stitches + 2)
Row I: I ch, I sc in each ch to end, turn.
Row 2: 2 ch, I hdc, *bring down 2 beads, 5 hdc, rep from * to end, turn.
Row 3: I ch, I dc in each hdc to end. Fasten off.

---

 62 DOUBLE MESH FRINGE
Directory view, page 25

Skill level: Beginner/easy

Cotton perle

METHOD

Make a foundation chain of the required length, or work row I directly into the item to be trimmed with right side facing.
(multiple of 4 stitches + I)
Row I: I sc in 2nd ch from hook, I sc in each ch to end, turn.
Row 2: I ch, I sc in same st, 3 ch, skip 3 sc, I sc in next sc, turn.
Rows 3–4: As row 2. Fasten off.
Fringe: Insert 2 pairs of strands of prepared fringe yarn into each 3-ch sp on the final row.

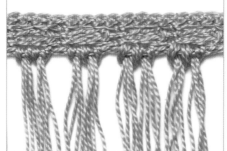

---

 63 GRANNY FRINGE
Directory view, page 25

Skill level: Beginner/easy

Cotton perle

METHOD

Make a foundation chain of the required length, or work row I directly into the item to be trimmed with right side facing.
(multiple of 7 stitches + I)
Row I: I sc in 2nd ch from hook, I sc in each ch to end, turn.
Row 2: 3 ch, *2 dc, I ch, skip I sc, I dc in next sc, 2 ch, skip 2 sc, I dc in next sc, rep from * to end, turn.
Row 3: 3 ch, *2 ch, I dc in next dc, I ch, I dc in each of next 3 dc, rep from * to end, turn.
Fringe: Insert 2 strands of the prepared fringe yarn into each ch sp on the final row to end.

BRAIDS

SEE ALSO

Standard crochet abbreviations, page 125
Refresher course, pages 110–125

64 LIGHT AND DARK
Directory view, page 26

Skill level: Beginner/easy

Worked in cotton perle in two colors: A and B

METHOD

Using yarn A make a foundation chain of the required length, or work row 1 directly into the item to be trimmed with right side facing. (odd number of stitches)

Row 1: (A) 1 ch, 1 sc in each st or position to end, turn.

Row 2: (A and B together) 1 ch, *skip 1 st, 2 dc in next st, rep from * to end. Fasten off yarn A only.

Row 3: (B only) As row 1. Fasten off.

65 SHINY SHELLS
Directory view, page 26

Skill level: Beginner/easy

Cotton perle

10 mm shell-shaped sequins in a range of colors

METHOD

Thread the sequins onto the yarn before beginning.

Make a foundation chain of the required length, or work row 1 directly into the item to be trimmed with right side facing. (multiple of 4 stitches + 1)

Row 1: 1 ch, 1 sc in each st or position to end, turn.

Row 2: 1 ch, *bring down sequin in next sc, 3 sc, rep from * to end, turn.

Row 3: As row 1. Fasten off.

66 FANS AND COLUMNS

Directory view, page 26

Skill level: Beginner/easy

 Cotton perle

METHOD

Make a foundation chain of the required length, or work row 1 directly into the item to be trimmed with right side facing. (multiple of 10 stitches + 5)
Row 1: 1 ch, 1 sc in each st or position to end, turn.
Row 2: 3 ch, 4 dc, *skip 2 sts, 5 dc in next st, 2 ch, skip 2 sts, 5 dc, rep from * to end. Fasten off.

67 FANS BRAID

Directory view, page 26

Skill level: Beginner/easy

 Cotton perle

METHOD

Make a foundation chain of the required length, or work row 1 directly into the item to be trimmed with right side facing. (multiple of 3 stitches + 1)
Row 1: 1 ch, 1 sc in each st or position to end, turn.
Row 2: 1 ch, *2 ch, skip 2 sts, 1 sc, rep from * to end, turn.
Row 3: 3 ch, 3 dc in each 2-ch sp to end. Fasten off.

68 SOFT CENTER

Directory view, page 27

Skill level: Beginner/easy

 Worked in two yarns: cotton perle (smooth) and mohair (fluffy)

METHOD

Using the smooth yarn, make a foundation chain of the required length, or work row 1 directly into the item to be trimmed with right side facing. (odd number of stitches)
Row 1: (smooth yarn) 1 ch, 1 sc in each st or position to end. Fasten off, turn.
Row 2: (fluffy yarn) 3 ch, *2 dc in next st, 1 dc, rep from * to end, turn.
Row 3: (fluffy yarn) As row 1. Fasten off, turn.
Row 4: (smooth yarn) As row 1. Fasten off.

69 BLOCKS BRAID

Directory view, page 27

Skill level: Beginner/easy

 Worked in cotton perle in two colors: A and B

METHOD

Using yarn A, make a foundation chain of the required length, or work row 1 directly into the item to be trimmed with right side facing. (multiple of 3 stitches + 1)
Row 1: (A) 2 ch, 1 hdc in each st or position to end. Fasten off, turn.
Row 2: (B) 2 ch, *2 hdc into next st, 1ch, skip 1 st, 1 hdc in next st, rep from * to end. Fasten off, turn.
Row 3: (A) 1 ch, 1 sc in each st to end. Fasten off.

70 ## MOVING BLOCKS
Directory view, page 27

Skill level: Intermediate

 *Cotton perle*

METHOD

Make a foundation chain of the required length, or work row I directly into the item to be trimmed with right side facing. (multiple of 8 stitches + I)
Row I: 5 ch, I dc in 9th ch from hook, 5 dc, *2 ch, skip 2 sts, 6 dc, rep from * to end, turn.
Row 2: As row I. Fasten off.

---

71 ## FINE BLOCKS
Directory view, page 27

Skill level: Intermediate

Cotton perle

METHOD

Make a foundation chain of the required length, or work row I directly into the item to be trimmed with right side facing. (multiple of 13 stitches + 3)
Row I: 4 ch, I dc in 7th ch from hook, 5 dc, (I ch, skip I st, I dc) 3 times, I ch, *skip I st, 6 dc, (I ch, skip I st, I dc) 3 times, I ch, rep from * to last st, I dc, turn.
Row 2: 4 ch, *(skip I st, I dc, I ch in next st) 3 times, I ch, 6 dc, rep from * to last 2 sts, I ch, skip I st, I dc in last st. Fasten off.

---

72 ## LAZY FANS
Directory view, page 27

Skill level: Intermediate

Cotton perle

METHOD

Make a foundation chain of the required length, or work row I directly into the item to be trimmed with right side facing. (multiple of 7 stitches + I)
Row I: I ch, *2 sc, skip I st, 4 dc in next st, skip I st, 2 sc, rep from * to end. Fasten off.

---

73 ## WAVES BRAID
Directory view, page 27

Skill level: Intermediate

Cotton perle

METHOD

Make a foundation chain of the required length, or work row I directly into the item to be trimmed with right side facing. (multiple of 12 stitches)
Row I: 3 ch, I dc in same st, *3 dc, dc2tog twice, 3 dc, 2 dc in next st twice, rep from * to end. The last rep will end with only one 2 dc in next st. Fasten off.

74 BOBBLES BRAID
Directory view, page 28

Skill level: Intermediate

 *Cotton perle*

METHOD

Notes: bobble = dc4tog in next st.
Make a foundation chain of the required length, or work row 1 directly into the item to be trimmed with right side facing. (multiple of 7 stitches + 1)
Row 1: 1 ch, 1 sc in each st or position to end, turn.
Row 2: 3 ch, *2 dc, skip 1 st, bobble, skip 1 st, 2 dc, rep from * to end, turn.
Row 3: As row 1. Fasten off.

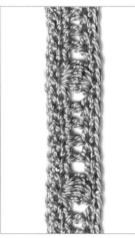

75 RANDOM BOBBLES
Directory view, page 28

Skill level: Intermediate

 *Cotton perle*

METHOD

Notes: bobble = dc4tog in next st.
Make a foundation chain of the required length, or work row 1 directly into the item to be trimmed with right side facing. (multiple of 6 stitches + 3)
Row 1: 1 ch, 1 sc in each st or position to end, turn.
Row 2: 1 ch, *2 sc, bobble, 3 sc, rep from * to end, turn.
Row 3: As row 1.
Row 4: As row 2, but place bobbles at random. Fasten off.

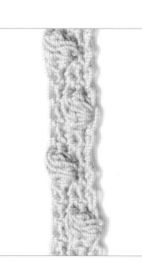

76 JAZZY BRAID
Directory view, page 28

Skill level: Beginner/easy

 *Cotton perle*

5 mm glass seed beads

METHOD

Thread the beads onto the yarn before beginning.
Make a foundation chain of the required length, or work row 1 directly into the item to be trimmed with right side facing. (multiple of 3 stitches + 1)
Row 1: 1 ch, *bring down a bead to work into next sc, 2 sc, rep from * to end. Fasten off.

77 RIDGE BRAID
Directory view, page 28

Skill level: Intermediate

Cotton perle

METHOD

Notes: bobble = dc4tog in next st.
Make a foundation chain of the required length, or work row 1 directly into the item to be trimmed with right side facing. (multiple of 6 stitches + 1)
Row 1: 1 ch, 1 sc in each st or position to end, turn.
Row 2: 1 ch, *bobble, 5 sc, rep from * to end, turn.
Row 3: As row 1. Fasten off.

78 **STRIPED BRAID**
Directory view, page 28

Skill level: Intermediate

 *Worked in cotton perle in three colors: A, B, and C*

METHOD

Using color A, make a foundation chain of the required length, or work row I directly into the item to be trimmed with right side facing. (any number of stitches)
Row I: (A) I ch, I sc in each st or position to end. Fasten off, turn.
Row 2: (B) As row I.
Row 3: (C) As row I.
Row 4: (A) As row I.

---

79 **SPRAY BRAID**
Directory view, page 28

Skill level: Beginner/easy

Worked in cotton perle in two colors: A and B

METHOD

Using color A make a foundation chain of the required length, or work row I directly into the item to be trimmed with right side facing. (any number of stitches)
Row I: (A) I ch, I sc in each st or position to end, turn.
Row 2: (A) 2 ch, I hdc in each st to end. Fasten off, turn.
Row 3: (B) I ch, *I dc into sc on row I, I sc, rep from * to last st, I dc, turn.
Row 4: (B) As row I. Fasten off, turn.
Row 5: (A) As row 3, working dc into dc on row 3.
Row 6: (A) As row I. Fasten off.

---

80 **EYELET BRAID**
Directory view, page 29

Skill level: Intermediate

Cotton perle

METHOD

Make a foundation chain of the required length, or work row I directly into the item to be trimmed with right side facing. (multiple of 8 stitches + I)
Row I: I ch, I sc in each st or position to end, turn.
Row 2: 3 ch, *(I ch, skip I st, I dc in next st) 3 times, 2 dc, rep from * to end, turn.
Row 3: As row I. Fasten off.

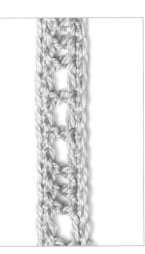

 **81** **LAYER BRAID**
Directory view, page 29

Skill level: Intermediate

Worked in cotton perle in two colors: A and B

METHOD

Using color A, make a foundation chain of the required length, or work row I directly into the item to be trimmed with right side facing. (odd number of stitches)
Row I: (A) I ch, I sc in each st or position to end. Fasten off, turn.
Row 2: (B) 3 ch, *I dc in each st to end, turn.
Row 3: (B) As row I. Fasten off, turn.
Row 4: (A) I ch, *I sc, I dc in next st on row 2, rep from * to end. Fasten off.

82 BOBBLE STEPS

Directory view, page 29

Skill level: Intermediate

 *Worked in cotton perle in two colors: A and B*

METHOD

Notes: bobble = dc4tog in next st.
Using color A, make a foundation chain of the required length, or work row 1 directly into the item to be trimmed with right side facing. (multiple of 8 stitches + 1)
Row 1: (A) 1 ch, 1 sc in each st or position to end. Fasten off, turn.
Row 2: (B) 1 ch, *bobble, 7 sc, rep from * to end, turn.
Row 3: (B) As row 1. Do not fasten off.
Row 4: (B) 1 ch, *3 sc, bobble, 4 sc, rep from * to end, turn.
Row 5: (B) As row 1. Do not fasten off.
Row 6: (B) 1 ch, *6 sc, bobble, 1 sc, rep from * to end, turn.
Row 7: (B) As row 1.
Row 8: (A) As row 1. Fasten off.

83 PYRAMIDS BRAID

Directory view, page 29

Skill level: Intermediate

 Cotton perle

METHOD

Make a foundation chain of the required length, or work row 1 directly into the item to be trimmed with right side facing. (multiple of 6 + 1 stitches)
Row 1: 1 ch, 1 sc in each st or position to end, turn.
Row 2: 1 ch, 1 sc in first st *6 ch, 1 sc in 2nd ch from hook, 1 sc in next ch, 1 hdc in next ch, 1 dc in next ch, 1 tr in next ch, 1 dtr in last of the 6 ch, skip 5 ch on row 1, 1 sc in next sc, rep from * to end. Fasten off.

84 SHEATHS BRAID

Directory view, page 29

Skill level: Intermediate

 *Cotton perle*

METHOD

Make a foundation chain of the required length, or work row 1 directly into the item to be trimmed with right side facing. (multiple of 7 + 4 chains)
Row 1: Working along one side of the foundation chain only, 1 sc in 2nd ch from hook, 1 sc in each of next 2 ch, *3 ch, skip 3 ch, 1 sc in each of next 4 ch, rep from * to end.
Row 2: Working along the other side of the foundation chain, 3 ch, *3 ch, 5 dc in next 3-ch loop, rep from * to last 3 sc, 1 ch, 1 dc in last st. Fasten off.

85 LONG WAVES

Directory view, page 30

Skill level: Intermediate

Cotton perle

METHOD

Make a foundation chain of the required length, or work row 1 directly into the item to be trimmed with right side facing. (multiple of 12 stitches)
Row 1: 1 ch, *1 sc, 2 hdc, 2 dc, 2 tr, 2 dc, 2 hdc, 1 sc, rep from * to end, turn.
Row 2: 1 ch, 1 sc in each st to end, turn.
Row 3: 4 ch, *2 dc, 2 hdc, 2 sc, 2 hdc, 2 dc, 1 tr, rep from * to end. Fasten off.

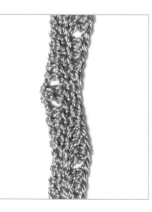

86 ANGLED CHEVRONS

Directory view, page 30

Skill level: Intermediate

Cotton perle

2 mm glass seed beads

METHOD

Thread the beads onto the yarn before starting work.
Make a foundation chain of the required length, or work row 1 directly into the item to be trimmed with right side facing. (multiple of 14 stitches + 1)
Row 1: 1 ch, 2 sc in 2nd ch from hook, *1 sc in each of next 8 ch, skip 1 ch, 1 sc in each of next 4 ch, 3 dc into next ch, rep from * to end, omitting 1 sc at end of last rep, turn
Row 2: 1 ch, 2 sc in first sc, *1 sc into each of next 3 sc, bring down 1 bead to work into next sc, skip 1 sc, bring down 1 bead to work into next sc, 1 sc in each of next 8 sc, 3 sc into next ch, rep from * to last long section of chevron, end with 2 sc in last st. Fasten off.

87 SHALLOW FILET BRAID
Directory view, page 30

Skill level: Intermediate

Cotton perle

METHOD

Make a foundation chain of the required length, or work row 1 directly into the item to be trimmed with right side facing. (multiple of 5 stitches + 1)
Row 1: 1 ch, 1 sc in each st or position to end, turn.
Row 2: As row 1.
Row 3: 3 ch, *4 ch, skip 4 ch, 1 dc in next sc, rep from * to end.
Row 4: As row 1.
Row 5: As row 1. Fasten off.

89 DEEP FILET BRAID
Directory view, page 30

Skill level: Intermediate

Cotton perle

METHOD

Make a foundation chain of the required length, or work row 1 directly into the item to be trimmed with right side facing. (multiple of 6 stitches + 1)
Row 1: 1 ch, 1 sc in each st or position to end, turn.
Rows 2 & 3: As row 1.
Row 4: 1 ch, 1 sc in first st, *3 ch, skip 2 sc, 1 sc in next sc, rep from * to end, turn.
Row 5: *2 ch, 1 sc in next 3-ch loop, rep from * to last st, 1 sc, turn.
Row 6: 1 ch, 1 sc in each st to end, turn.
Row 7: As row 6. Fasten off.

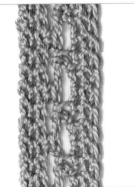

90 LUXURIOUS BRAID
Directory view, page 30

Skill level: challenging/complex

Cotton perle

METHOD

Make a foundation chain of the required length, or work row 1 directly into the item to be trimmed with right side facing. (multiple of 3 stitches + 1)
Row 1: 1 ch, 1 sc in each st or position to end, turn.
Row 2: As row 1.
Row 3: 1 ch, *3 sc, 4 ch, rep from * to end omitting 4 ch on last rep, turn.
Row 4: 1 ch, *3 sc, 8 dc in 4-ch loop, *rep from * to last 3 sts, 3 sc. Fasten off.
Return to the beginning of foundation row, rep rows 1–4. Fasten off.

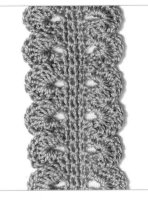

MOTIFS

SEE ALSO

*Standard crochet abbreviations,
page 125
Refresher course,
pages 110–125*

 **SUN DAISY**
Directory view, page 31

Skill level: Beginner/easy

 Cotton perle

METHOD

Notes: dc2tog = work 1 dc into each of next 2 dc until 1 loop of each remains on hook, yo and through all 3 loops on hook.
Make 6 ch, sl st into first ch to form a ring.
Round 1: 1 ch, 15 sc in ring, sl st into first sc.
Round 2: (3 ch, dc2tog, 3 ch, sl st into next dc) 5 times, placing last sl st into last dc of previous round. Fasten off.

 **GOLDEN PANSY**
Directory view, page 31

Skill level: Beginner/easy

Cotton perle

METHOD

Notes: tr2tog in next st = work 2 tr in next st until 1 loop of each remains on hook, yo and through all 4 loops on hook.
Make 5 ch, sl st into first ch to form a ring.
Round 1: 1 ch, 12 sc into ring, sl st into first sc.
Round 2: 4 ch, tr2tog in next st, 4 ch, sl st into each of next 2 dc, rep from * 3 times, omitting 1 sl st at end of last rep.
Make stalk: 7 ch, 1 sc into 2nd ch from hook, 1 sc into each of next 5 ch. Fasten off.

92 SUNBURST

Directory view, page 31

Skill level: Beginner/easy

Cotton perle

METHOD

Make 6 ch, sl st into first ch to form a ring.
Round 1: 1 ch, (1 sc, 12 ch) 12 times into ring, sl st into first sc. Fasten off.

93 CLOVER
Directory view, page 31

Skill level: Beginner/easy

Cotton perle

METHOD

Notes: tr3tog = work 1 tr into each of same place as last st and the next 2 sc until 1 loop of each remains on hook, yo and through all 4 loops on hook.
Make 5 ch, sl st into first ch to form a ring.
Round 1: 1 ch, 10 sc into ring, sl st into first sc.
Round 2: 1 ch, 1 sc into first dc, *4 ch, tr3tog, 4 ch, 1 sc in same place as last st, 1 sc in next sc, rep from * twice.
Make stalk: 7 ch (or number required), turn, 1 sc in 2nd ch from hook, 1 sc in each ch, sl st in first sc on round. Fasten off.

94 IRISH SHAMROCK
Directory view, page 31

Skill level: Intermediate

Cotton perle

METHOD

Make 6 ch, sl st into first ch to form a ring.
Round 1: 1 ch, 18 sc into ring, sl st into first sc.
Round 2: 8 ch, skip 4 sc, sl st in next sc, 10 ch, skip 4 sc, sl st into next sc, 8 ch, sl st in next 2 sc.
Make stalk: 12 ch, 1 sc in 3rd ch from hook, 1 sc into each of next 9 ch, sl st into last sc.
Round 3: 16 sc in next 8-ch loop, 20 sc in next 10-ch loop, 16 sc in next 8-ch loop, sl st to beg of stalk. Fasten off.

LINKED PETALS
Directory view, page 32

Skill level: Beginner/easy

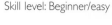 *Cotton perle*

METHOD

Notes: Bobble: dc4tog in next st = 4 dc into next sc until I loop of each remains on hook, yo and through all 5 loops.
Make 6 ch, sl st in to first ch to form a ring.
Round I: I ch, 14 sc in ring, sl st into first sc.
Round 2: 3 ch, bobble in next sc, 5 ch, *skip I sc, I bobble in next dc, 5 ch, rep from * to end, sl st in top of first bobble. Fasten off.

SUNSHINE
Directory view, page 32

Skill level: Intermediate

 *Cotton perle*

METHOD

Make 9 ch, sl st in first ch to form a ring.
Round I: I ch, 18 sc in ring, sl st into first sc.
Round 2: *9 ch, I sc in 4th ch from hook, I hdc in each of next 2 ch, I dc in each of next 3 ch, skip 2 sc on ring, sl st in next sc, rep from * to end, placing last st into same st as sl st of previous round. Fasten off.

ENGLISH ROSE
Directory view, page 32

Skill level: Intermediate

Cotton perle

METHOD

Make 8 ch, sl st into first ch to form a ring.
Round I: 3 ch, I dc in ring, (6 ch, 3 dc in ring) 5 times, 6 ch, I dc in ring, sl st in top of ch at beg of round.
Round 2: I ch, *(I sc, I hdc, 7 dc, I hdc, I sc), in next 6-ch loop, I ch, skip I dc, I sl st in next dc, rep from * 5 times, working last sl st in 3rd of 3 ch at beg of previous round. Fasten off.

IRISH LEAF
Directory view, page 32

Skill level: Beginner/easy

 Cotton perle

METHOD

Notes: Work into back loop only on each repeat of row 2.
Make 11 ch.
Row 1: Working into one loop only along first side of ch, 1 sc into 2nd ch from hook, 1 sc in each of next 8 ch, 3 sc in last ch, working in one loop only along other side of foundation ch, 1 sc in each of next 7 ch, turn.
Row 2: Working in back loop only, 1 ch, 1 sc in first sc, 1 sc in each of next 7 sc, 3 sc in next sc, 1 sc in each of next 7 sc, turn.
Rep row 2 as many times as desired.
Fasten off.

 PRINCELY PETALS
Directory view, page 32

Skill level: Intermediate

Cotton perle

METHOD

Round 1: 10 ch, sl st into first ch, (9 ch, sl st in same ch as last sl st) twice.
Round 2: *1 ch, (2 sc, 1 hdc, 11 dc, 1 hdc, 2 sc), in next 9-ch loop, 1 ch sl st into same sl st as first round, rep from * to end, sl st to first st. Fasten off.

 **FAN CIRCLE**
Directory view, page 33

Skill level: Beginner/easy

Fingering weight wool mixture

METHOD

Make 6 ch, sl st into first ch to form a ring.
Round 1: 6 ch, (3 tr in ring, 2 ch) 5 times, 2 tr in ring, sl st into 4th of 6 ch at beg of round.
Round 2: 1 ch, 1 sc in 2-ch loop, *6 ch, skip 3 tr, 1 sc in next 2-ch loop, rep from * to end, omitting sc at end of last rep, sl st in sc at beg of round.
Round 3: 1 ch, (1 sc, 1 hdc, 1 dc, 3 tr, 1 dc, 1 hdc, 1 sc) into each 6-ch loop, sl st in first sc. Fasten off.

SILHOUETTE CLOVER
Directory view, page 33

 Skill level: Intermediate

Cotton perle

METHOD

Round 1: 16 ch, sl st in first ch (first loop formed), (15 ch, sl st in same ch as last sl st) twice.

Round 2: 1 ch, (28 hdc in next loop, 1 sl st in same ch as sl st of first round) 3 times.

Make stalk: 12 ch, 1 hdc in 3rd ch from hook, 1 hdc in each ch to end, sl st in same ch as last sl st. Fasten off.

WESTERN MOTIF
Directory view, page 33

Skill level: Intermediate

Cotton perle

METHOD

Make 8 ch, sl st into first ch to form a ring.
Round 1: 1 ch, 15 sc in ring, sl st in first ch.
Round 2: 12 ch, skip 1 sc, *1 tr in next sc, 8 ch, rep from * to end, sl st in 4th of 12 ch.
Round 3: 1 ch, *(1 sc, 1 hdc,1 dc, 3 tr, 3 ch, sl st in 3rd ch from hook, 2 tr, 1 dc, 1 hdc, 1 sc) in 8-ch loop, rep from * to end, sl st in first ch. Fasten off.

LAYERED ROSE
Directory view, page 34

Skill level: Intermediate

Cotton perle

METHOD

Make 8 ch, sl st in first ch to form a ring.
Round 1: 1 ch, 18 sc, sl st in first ch.
Round 2: 6 ch, skip first 2 sc, *1 hdc in next sc, 4 ch, skip 2 dc, rep from * to end, sl st in 2nd of 6 ch at beg of round.
Round 3: 1 ch, (1 sc, 1 hdc, 3 dc, 1 hdc, 1 sc) in each 4-ch loop, sl st in first dc. (6 petals)
Round 4: sl st in back of the nearest hdc of 2nd round, *5 ch, working behind each petal of previous round sl st in next hdc of 2nd round, rep from * to end.
Round 5: 1 ch, (1 sc, 1 hdc, 5 dc, 1 hdc, 1 sc) in each 5-ch loop join with a sl st in first sc.
Round 6: sl st in back of sl st of 4th round, *6 ch, working behind each petal of previous round, sl st in next sl st of 4th round, rep from * to end.
Round 7: (1 sc, 1 hdc, 6 dc, 1 hdc, 1 sc) in each 6-ch loop, join with a sl st in first sc. Fasten off.

104 ELEGANT ROSE
Directory view, page 34

Skill level: Challenging/complex

Cotton perle

METHOD

Notes: Picot = make 3ch, sl st into first of these ch.
Make 8 ch, sl st in first ch to form a ring.
Round 1: 3 ch, 15 dc in ring, sl st in 3rd of 3 ch at beg of round.
Round 2: 5 ch, (1 dc in next dc, 2 ch) 15 times, sl st in 3rd in of 5 ch at beg of round.
Round 3: 1 ch, 3 sc in each of the 16 2-ch loops, sl st in first sc.
Round 4: 1 ch, 1 sc in same sc as the last sl st, *6 ch, skip 5 sc, 1 sc in next sc, rep from * 6 times, 6 ch, sl st in first sc.
Round 5: sl st in first 6-ch loop, 1 ch, (1 sc, 1 hdc, 6 dc, 1 hdc, 1 sc) in each of the 8 6-ch loops, sl st in first sc, (8 petals worked).
Round 6: 1 ch, working behind each petal of previous round, 1 sc in first sc on 4th round, *7 ch, 1 sc in next sc on 4th round, rep from * 6 times, 7 ch, sl st in first sc.

Round 7: sl st in first 7-ch loop, 1 ch, (1 sc, 1 hdc, 7 dc, 1 hdc, 1 sc) in each of the 8 7-ch loops, sl st in first sc.
Round 8: 1 ch, working behind each petal of previous round, 1 sc in first sc on 6th round, *8 ch, 1 sc in next sc on 6th round, rep from * 6 times, 8 ch, sl st in first sc.
Round 9: sl st in first 8-ch loop, 1 ch, (1 sc, 1 hdc, 3 dc, picot, 2 dc, picot, 3 dc, 1 hdc, 1 sc) in each of the 8 8-ch loops, sl st in first dc. Fasten off.

105 FLOWER SILHOUETTE
Directory view, page 34

Skill level: Intermediate

Cotton perle

METHOD

Make 20 ch, sl st in first ch to form a ring.
Round 1: 1 ch, 38 sc in ring, sl st in first sc.
Round 2: *9 ch, skip 6 sc, sl st in next sc, rep from * 4 times, sl st in each of next 3 sc.
Round 3: 2 sc in each 9-ch loop, 1 sc in each of next 3 sl st, sl st to first sc.
Round 4: 3 ch, 1 dc in each sc, sl st in first sc of round.
Make stem: 14 ch, 1 sc in 3rd ch from hook, 1 sc in each of next 11 ch. Fasten off.

EASTERN MOTIF
Directory view, page 35

Skill level: Intermediate

 Cotton perle

METHOD

Make 8 ch, sl st in first ch to form a ring.
Round 1: 1 ch, 16 sc in ring, sl st in first sc.
Round 2: 4 ch, 2 tr in first sc, 3 tr in next sc, 5 ch, (skip 2 sc, 3 tr in each of next 2 sc, 5 ch) 3 times, sl st in top of 4 ch at beg of round.
Round 3: 1 ch, *(1 hdc, 1 dc) in next tr, 2 tr in each of next 2 tr, (1 dc, 1 hdc) in next tr, 1 sc in next tr, 1 sc in each of next 2 ch, 3 sc in next ch, 1 sc in each of next 2 ch, 1 sc in next tr, rep from * 3 times, omit 1 sc at the end of last rep, sl st in first sc. Fasten off.

INTRICATE PETALS
Directory view, page 35

Skill level: Intermediate

Cotton perle

METHOD

Make 12 ch, sl st in first ch to form a ring.
Round 1: 1 ch, 24 sc in ring, sl st in first sc.
Round 2: 12 ch, *skip next sc, 1 sc in next sc, turn, 3 ch, 1 dc in each of first 7 ch of 12-ch arch, turn, 3 ch, skip first dc, 1 dc in each of next 6 dc, 1 dc in top of 3 ch (first block made), skip next sc on ring, ** 1 tr in next sc, 8 ch *, rep from * to * 4 times, and rep from * to ** once, sl st in 4th of 12 ch at beg of round. Fasten off.

ELEGANT PETALS
Directory view, page 35

Skill level: Challenging/complex

Cotton perle

METHOD

Notes: Picot = make 3 ch, sl st in first of these ch.
Make 6 ch, sl st in first ch to form a ring.
Round 1: 1 ch, 15 sc in ring, sl st in first ch.
Round 2: 1 ch, *2 sc, (1 sc, 9 ch, 1 sc) in next dc, 1 sc, rep from * to end, sl st in first sc.
Round 3: 1 ch, *1 sc, skip 1 sc, 21 dc in 9-ch loop, skip 1 sc, rep from * to end, sl st in first sc.
Round 4: 1 ch, *1 sc in sc of round 2, 5 ch, skip 5 dc, 1 sc in next dc, picot, 5 ch in first sc, skip 4 dc, 1 sc in next dc (middle dc in loop), picot, 5 ch, rep from * to end, sl st in first sc. Fasten off.

SHELL FLOWER
Directory view, page 35

Skill level: Intermediate

 Cotton perle

METHOD

Make 6 ch, sl st in first ch to form a ring.
Round 1: 3 ch, 15 dc in ring, sl st in 3rd of 3 ch at beg of round.
Round 2: 1 ch, 1 sc in same st, 1 sc in next dc, *(1 sc, 7 ch, 1 sc) in next dc, 1 sc in each of next 3 dc, rep from * 3 times, omitting 3 sc at end of last rep, sl st in first ch.
Round 3: 1 ch, 1 sc in same st, *(2 hdc, 17 dc, 2 hdc), in 7-ch loop, skip 2 sc, 1 sc in next sc, rep from * 3 times, omitting 1 sc at end of last rep, sl st in first sc. Fasten off.

 **TRELLIS MOTIF**
Directory view, page 36

Skill level: Intermediate

 *Cotton perle*

METHOD

Make 6 ch, sl st in first ch to form a ring.
Round 1: 3 ch, 15 dc in ring, sl st in 3rd of 3 ch at beg of round.
Round 2: 5 ch, 1 dc in same st, *1 ch, skip 1 dc, (1 dc, 2 ch, 1 dc), in next dc, rep from * 6 times, 1 ch, sl st in 3rd of 5 ch at beg of round.
Round 3: sl st in first 2-ch loop, 3 ch, (1 dc, 2 ch, 2 dc) in same loop, *1 ch, (2 dc, 2 ch, 2 dc), in next 2-ch loop, rep from * 6 times, 1 ch, sl st in 3rd of 3 ch at beg of round.
Round 4: sl st in next dc and first 2-ch loop, 3 ch, 6 dc in same loop, 1 sc in next 1-ch loop, (7 dc in next 2-ch loop, 1 sc in next 1-ch loop) 7 times, sl st in 3rd of 3 ch at beg of round. Fasten off.

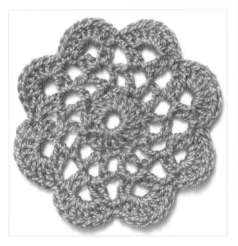

MARIGOLD
Directory view, page 36

Skill level: Beginner/easy

Cotton perle

METHOD

Notes: dtr3tog = 3 dtr in 2-ch loop until 1 loop of each remains on hook, yo and through all 4 loops on hook.
fpsc (front post sc) = work 1 sc around stem of next dc, inserting hook from right to left.
Make 4 ch, sl st in first ch to form a ring.
Round 1: 5 ch, (1 dc in ring, 2 ch) 5 times, sl st in 3rd of 5 ch at beg of round.
Round 2: 5 ch, *dtr3tog in 2-ch loop, 5 ch, 1fpsc around stem of next dc, 4 ch, rep from * 5 times, sl st in first ch of this round. Fasten off.

STAR FLOWER
Directory view, page 36

Skill level: Beginner/easy

Cotton perle

METHOD

Make 4 ch, sl st in first ch to form a ring.
Round 1: 3 ch, 15 dc in ring, sl st in 3rd of 5 ch at beg of round.
Round 2: 4 ch, (skip 1 dc, 1 sc in next st, 3 ch) 7 times, sl st into first ch at beg of round.
Round 3: 7 ch, (1 sc in next sc, 4 ch) 7 times, sl st in 3rd of 7 ch.
Round 4: 1 ch, *(1 sc, 1 hdc, 1 dc, 1 hdc, 1 sc) in each 4-ch loop, sl st in first ch.
Fasten off.

 **CIRCLED LACE**
Directory view, page 36

Skill level: Intermediate

Cotton perle

METHOD

Make 10 ch, sl st in first ch to form a ring.
Round 1: 3 ch, 23 dc in ring, sl st in 3rd of 5 ch at beg of round.
Round 2: 3 ch, (2 dc in next dc, 1 dc in each of next 2 dc) to end, omitting final dc, sl st in 3rd of 3 ch at beg of round.
Round 3: 3 ch, 1 dc in each of next 2 dc, 2 ch, 2 dc in next dc, *1 dc in each of next 3 dc, 2 ch, 2 dc in next dc, rep from * to end, sl st in 3rd of 3 ch at beg of round.
Round 4: 3 ch, 1 dc in each of next 2 dc, *2 ch, 1 dc in next 2-ch loop, 2 ch, 1 dc in each of next 5 dc, rep from * to end, omitting final 3 dc, sl st in 3rd of 3 ch at beg of round.
Round 5: 3 ch, 1 dc in next dc, *5 ch, skip 1 dc, 1 dc in next dc, 5 ch, skip 1 dc, 1 dc in each of next 3 dc, rep from * to end, omitting 2 dc at end of last rep, sl st into 3rd of 3 ch at beg of round. Fasten off.

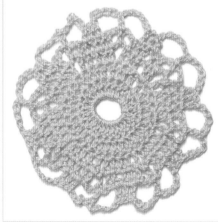

 **FRAMED FLOWER**
Directory view, page 37

Skill level: Intermediate

Cotton perle

METHOD

Make 12 ch, sl st in first ch to form a ring.
Round 1: 1 ch, 24 sc in ring, sl st in first sc.
Round 2: 12 ch, skip next sc, 1 sc in next sc, turn, 3 ch, 1 dc in each of first 7 ch, turn, 3 ch, 1 dc in each of next 6 dc, 1 dc in top of 3 ch, (first block made), *skip next sc in ring, 1 tr in next sc, 8 ch, skip next sc, 1 sc in next sc, turn, 3 ch, 1 dc in each of first 7 ch, turn, 3 ch, 1 dc in each of next 6 dc, 1 dc in top of 3 ch for next block. Rep from * 4 times, sl st in fourth of 12 ch at beg of round.
Round 3: sl st to top of 3 ch at corner of first block, 1 ch, 1 sc into top of 3 ch, 13 ch, *1 sc in 3rd of 3 ch at top of next block, 13 ch, rep from * to end, sl st in first sc.
Round 4: 1 ch, 1 sc in each st to end.
Fasten off.

 ## SQUARE FRAMED CIRCLES
Directory view, page 37

Skill level: Intermediate

 *Cotton perle*

METHOD

Make 6 ch, sl st in first ch to form a ring.
Round 1: 3 ch, 15 dc in ring, sl st in 3rd of 3 ch at beg of round.
Round 2: 1 ch, 1 sc into same st, 1 sc in next dc, *(1 sc, 7 ch, 1 sc) in next dc, 1 sc in each of next 3 dc, rep from * 3 times, omitting 2 sc at end of last rep, sl st in first sc.
Round 3: 1 ch, 1 sc in same st, *(2 hdc, 17 dc, 2 hdc) in next 7-ch loop, skip 2 sc, 1 sc in next sc, rep from * 3 times, omitting 1 sc at end of last rep, sl st in first dc.
Round 4: sl st in each of next 2 hdc and 6 dc, 1 ch, 1 sc in same st, 9 ch, skip 5 dc, 1 sc in next dc, *7 ch, 1 sc in sixth dc of next loop, 9 ch, skip 5 dc, 1 sc in next dc, rep from * to end, 7 ch, sl st in first sc.
Round 5: 3 ch, *(8 dc, 1 tr, 8 dc) in 9-ch loop, 1 dc in next sc, 7 dc in next 7-ch loop, 1 dc in next sc, rep from * 3 times, omitting 1 dc at end of last rep, sl st in 3rd ch at beg of round. Fasten off.

PINWHEEL
Directory view, page 37

Skill level: Beginner/easy

 *Cotton perle*

METHOD

Make 6 ch, sl st in first ch to form a ring.
Round 1: 3 ch, 2 dc in ring, (2 ch, 3 dc in ring) 5 times, 2 ch, sl st in top of 3 ch.
Round 2: sl st in next 2 dc and 2-ch loop, 4 ch, (2 tr, 2 ch, 3 tr) in 2-ch loop, (3 tr, 2 ch, 3 tr) in each 2-ch loop to end, sl st in top of 4 ch. Fasten off.

CHRYSANTHEMUM
Directory view, page 38

Skill level: Beginner/easy

Cotton perle   *1 pin back for fastening*

METHOD

Make 21 ch, 1 sl st in 2nd ch from hook, 1 sl st in each ch to end, turn, *skip first st, sl st in each of next 2 sts, 17 ch, skip first ch, sl st in each ch to end, turn *, rep from * to * until approximately 60 to 70 petals have been completed. Fasten off.
To make up: Beginning at one end of the work, fold the base of the petals round and round and secure with sewing stitches, forming a slight spiral at the very beginning. Continue until all of the petals have been secured.
Attach to the pin backing if required.

118 CHAIN FLOWER

Directory view, page 38

Skill level: Beginner/easy

Cotton perle in two colors

5 mm glass seed beads in two colors
1 pin back for fastening

METHOD

This flower consists of 2 circles in different colors.

First (back) circle: Make 5 ch, sl st in first ch to form a ring.

Round 1: 1 ch, 15 sc in ring, sl st in first sc.

Round 2: *4 ch, sl st in next sc, rep from * to end.

Round 3: sl st in each of first 2 ch of next loop, sl st in center of same loop, 5 ch, *sl st in center of next 4-ch loop, 5 ch, rep from * to end, sl st in sl st at center of first loop.

Round 4: sl st in each of first 3 ch of next loop, sl st in center of same loop, 6 ch, *sl st in center of next 5-ch loop, 6 ch, rep from * to end, sl st in sl st at center of first loop.

Round 5: sl st in each of first 3 ch of next loop, sl st in center of same loop, 7 ch, *sl st in center of next 6-ch loop, 7 ch, rep from * to end, sl st in sl st at center of first loop.

Second (front) circle: Make 5 ch, sl st in first ch to form a ring.

Round 1: 1 ch, 20 sc in ring, sl st in first sc.

Rounds 2–5: Complete as for first circle. Fasten off.

To make up: Place the larger circle over the smaller and stitch the centers together. Thread two separate batches of 10 beads onto thread and sew to the center of the front circle. Attach to a pin backing as required.

119 GOLDEN LEAF

Directory view, page 38

Skill level: Challenging/complex

Cotton perle

METHOD

Make 5 ch, sl st in first ch to form a ring.

Round 1: 1 sc in ring, *14 ch, 1 dc in 6th ch from hook, (2 ch, skip 2 ch, 1 dc in next ch) twice, 2 ch, 1 sc in ring *, ^ 17 ch, 1 dc in 6th ch from hook, (2 ch, skip 2 ch, 1 dc in next ch) 3 times, 2 ch, 1 sc in ring ^, 20 ch, 1 dc in 6th ch from hook, (2 ch, skip 2 ch, 1 dc in next ch) 4 times, 2 ch, 1 sc in ring, rep from ^ to ^ once and from * to * once.

Round 2: 1 ch, 2 sc in next 2-ch loop, 1 hdc in base of next dc, (3 dc in next 2-ch loop, 1 dc in base of next dc), (3 dc in next 2-ch loop, 1 dc, 1 hdc in base of next dc), 3 sc in next 5-ch loop, (1 hdc, 1 dc) in next dc, (3 dc in next 2-ch loop, 1 dc in next dc), (3 dc in next 2-ch loop, 1 hdc in next dc), 2 sc in next 2-ch loop, 1 sc in next sc, (first section of leaf), 2 sc in next 2-ch loop, 1 hdc in base of next dc, (3 dc in next 2-ch loop, 1 dc in base of next dc) twice, (3 dc in next 2-ch loop, 1 dc, 1 hdc in base of next dc), 3 sc in next 5-ch loop, (1 hdc, 1 dc) in next dc, (3 dc in next 2-ch loop, 1 dc in next dc) twice, (3 dc in next 2-ch loop, 1 hdc in next dc), 2 sc in next 2-ch loop, 1 sc in next sc, [2nd section of leaf], 2 sc in next 2-ch loop, 1 hdc in base of next dc, (3 dc in next 2-ch loop, 1 dc in base of next dc) three times, (3 dc in next 2-ch loop, 1 dc, 1 hdc in base of next dc), 3 sc in next 5-ch loop, (1 hdc, 1 dc) in next dc, (3 dc in next 2-ch loop, 1 dc in next dc) three times, (3 dc in next 2-ch loop, 1 hdc in next dc), 2 sc in next 2-ch loop, 1 sc in next sc, [3rd section of leaf], repeat 2nd section of leaf and then first section of leaf, sl st in first sc.

Round 3: 1 ch, 1 sc in each st all the way round the leaf.

Make stem: 8 ch, 1 sc in 2nd ch from hook, 1 sc in each rem ch, sl st into first ch. Fasten off.

120 LAZY FROG
Directory view, page 38

Skill level: Beginner/easy

Cotton perle

Novelty lazy frog button

METHOD

Make 5 ch, sl st in first ch to form a ring.
Round 1: 1 ch, 10 sc in ring, sl st in first sc.
Round 2: 1 ch, 1 sc in each sc, sl st in first sc.
Round 3: 2 ch, skip 1st sc, 2 hdc in each of next 9 sc, 1 hdc in first st of round 2, sl st in 2nd of 2 ch.
Round 4: *2 ch, 2 dc in each of next 3 hdc, 2 ch, sl st in next hdc, rep from * 4 times, placing last st in 2nd of 2 ch on round 2. Fasten off.
Making up: Attach the lazy frog button to the center of this flower.

121 TUFTED FLOWER
Directory view, page 39

Skill level: Beginner/easy

Cotton perle

1 pin back for fastening

METHOD

Make 6 ch, sl st in first ch to form a ring.
Round 1: 1 ch, 20 sc in ring, join with sl st in first ch.
Round 2: 3 ch, 1 dc in same st, 2 dc in each sc to end, sl st in 3rd of 3 ch at beg of round.
Rounds 3–4: As Round 2.
Round 5: 1 ch, 1 sc in each of next 9 sts, insert hook from front to back in next st, skip next 9 sts, insert hook from front to back in next st, yo and draw through first 2 loops on hook, yo and draw through both loops on hook, *1 sc in each of next 10 sts, insert hook from front to back in next st, skip next 9 sts, insert hook from back to front in next st, yo and draw through first 2 loops on hook, yo and draw through both loops on hook, rep from * to end. Fasten off.
To make up: Make the tufted center by cutting 40 lengths of yarn, each approx 3 inches (7.5 cm) long, firmly bind together around the center with another piece of yarn. Fold the lengths in half and sew this bound section into the center of the flower.
Making up: Attach to the pin backing as required.

122 CONICAL SHELL
Directory view, page 39

Skill level: Beginner/easy

Cotton perle

METHOD

Make 29 ch.
Row 1: 2 sc in 2nd ch from hook, 2 sc in next ch, 2 hdc in next ch, 2 dc in each of next 22 ch, 2 hdc in next ch, 2 sc in last 2 ch. Fasten off.
Twist trim to form a circle and secure with some sewing stitches. This pattern can be made using trebles to give greater depth.

123 PEARL ROSE
Directory view, page 39

Skill level: Beginner/easy

🌀 *Cotton perle*

◗ *4 x 10 mm pearl buttons*
  1 pin back for fastening

METHOD

Make 6 ch, sl st in first ch to form a ring.

Round 1: 1 ch, 17 sc in ring, sl st in first ch.

Round 2: 5 ch, skip next 2 sc, *1 sc in next sc, 4 ch, skip next 2 sc, rep from * to end, sl st in 2nd of 5 ch at beg of round.

Round 3: *(1 sc, 1 hdc, 5 dc, 1 hdc, 1 sc) in next 4-ch loop, rep from * to end, sl st in first sc.

Round 4: *5 ch, pass these chs behind next group of sts, 1 sc in next sc of round 2, inserting the hook from behind, rep from * to end.

Round 5: *(1 sc, 1 hdc, 10 dc, 1 hdc, 1 sc) in next 5-ch loop, rep from * to end, sl st in first sc.

Round 6: *7 ch, pass these ch behind next group of sts, 1 sc in next sc of round 4, inserting the hook from behind, rep from * to end.

Round 7: *(1 sc, 1 hdc, 15 dc, 1 hdc, 1 sc) in next 7-ch loop, rep from * to end, sl st in first sc.

Round 8: *8 ch, pass these ch behind next group of sts, 1 sc in next sc of 6th round inserting the hook from behind, rep from * to end.

Round 9: *(1 sc, 1 hdc, 5 dc, 10 tr, 5 dc, 1 hdc, 1 sc) in next 7-ch loop, rep from * to end, sl st in first sc. Fasten off.

Making up: Arrange and sew the 4 pearl buttons in the center of the flower and attach to the pin backing as required.

124 SNOWFLAKE
Directory view, page 39

Skill level: Beginner/easy

🌀 *Cotton perle*

METHOD

Make 8 ch, sl st in first ch to form a ring.

Round 1: 2 ch, 17 hdc in ring, join in top of 2 ch at beg of round.

Round 2: 1 ch, 1 sc in same st, *17 ch, 1 sc in each of next 3 sts, rep from * 5 times, ending last rep with sc in next 2 sts, sl st in first sc.

Round 3: 1 ch, 1 sc in same st, *23 sc in next 17-ch loop, 1 sc in each of next 2 sc, 7 ch, sl st in same sc, 1 sc in next sc, rep from * 5 times, ending last rep with 7 ch, sl st in same dc, sl st in first sc. Fasten off.

ACCESSORIES

SEE ALSO

Standard crochet abbreviations, page 125
Refresher course, pages 110–125

 125 **RING BUTTON 1**
Directory view, page 40

Skill level: Beginner/easy

Cotton perle

Metal or plastic button ring of the required size

To fasten into buttonholes on a garment or to add decoration

METHOD

Notes: For this trim you will need a metal or plastic ring of the required size. Always insert the hook into the ring.

Row 1: Sl st in ring, hold in place, make a ch long enough to reach across the center area (this will make the bar to sew and secure the button). 3 ch, then dc around half of the ring, hold the securing bar in place, continue to work around the ring until it is completely covered. Fasten off.

126 **RING BUTTON 2**
Directory view, page 40

Skill level: Beginner/easy

Cotton perle

Metal or plastic button ring of the required size

To fasten into buttonholes on a garment or to add decoration

METHOD

Notes: For this trim you will need a metal or plastic ring of the required size. Always insert the hook into the ring.

Row 1: Sl st into ring, hold in place, make a ch long enough to reach across the center area (this will make the bar to sew and secure the button). 1 ch, then sc around half of the ring, hold the securing bar in place, continue to work around the ring until it is completely covered. Fasten off.

127 RING BUTTON 3

Directory view, page 40

Skill level: Beginner/easy

Cotton perle

Metal or plastic button ring of the required size

To fasten into buttonholes on a garment or to add decoration

METHOD

Notes: For this you need a metal or plastic ring of the required size. Always insert the hook into the ring.

Row 1: Sl st in ring, hold in place, make a ch long enough to reach across the center area (this will make the bar to sew and secure the button). 1 ch, then sc around half of the ring, hold the securing bar in place, continue to work around the ring until it is completely covered. Do not fasten off.

To complete button: Twist the tops of all the stitches to the inside of the ring and, using a yarn needle, fill in the center of the button by darning, weaving, or using any decorative stitches. Fasten off.

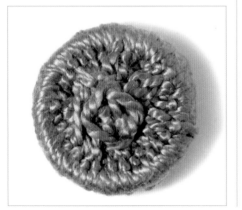

128 BALL BUTTON

Directory view, page 40

Skill level: Beginner/easy

Cotton perle

To fasten into buttonholes on a garment or to add decoration

METHOD

Notes: The covering for this type of button should be made a little small and the button should be firmly stuffed with yarn or suitable batting.

Make 2 ch.

Round 1: 6 sc in 2nd ch from hook, sl st in first sc.

Round 2: 1 ch, 2 sc in each sc, sl st in first sc.

Round 3: 1 ch, 1 sc in each sc, sl st in first sc. (This completes the first half of this spherical button. Sew in the loose yarn at the beginning of round 1).

Round 4: 1 ch, (1 sc, skip 1 sc) 6 times, sl st in first sc.

Insert some filling material into the center to pack out the button.

Round 5: 1 ch, (1 sc, skip 1 sc) 3 times, sl st in first sc.

Fasten off leaving sufficient length to close the base of the button and attach it to the garment.

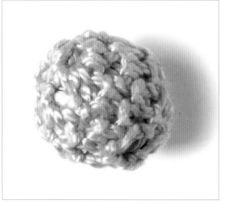

129 COVERED BUTTON

Directory view, page 40

Skill level: Intermediate

Cotton perle

Buttons used: self cover metal button forms

To fasten into buttonholes on a garment or to add decoration

METHOD

Notes: The covering for this type of button should be made a little small, to allow it to stretch to fit the metal button form.

Using a 5 inch (12.5 cm) length of yarn from the ball, wrap this around your finger and ease the circle free.

Round 1: Into this circle work 1 ch, 8 sc, holding firmly in fingers, gently pull the ends of this circle to tighten the ring, join with sl st in first sc.

Round 2: 1 ch, 1 sc in same st, 2 sc in each sc to end, sl st in first sc.

Round 3: 1 ch, *2 sc in next sc, 1 sc in next sc, rep from * to end, sl st in first sc. Increase on following rounds to required size.

Next round: 1 ch, 1 sc in each sc to end, sl st in first sc. Fasten off.

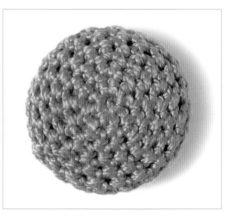

FLORAL BUTTONHOLE
Directory view, page 40

Skill level: Challenging/complex

 Cotton perle   *To create an unusual and decorative buttonhole*

METHOD

Notes: The button forms the center of the flower. This design suits a wide band.
Make a foundation chain of the required width of button band. You may need to adjust the position of the buttonholes to suit your garment.
Row 1: 1 ch, 1 sc in each st to end, turn. Work as many rows of sc as required.
Buttonhole row: Place buttonholes as required, by making 2 ch, skip 2 sc, near the center of the width of the band.
Next row: Work in sc, with 2 sc in the 2-chain loop.
Repeat the buttonhole row, next row, and rows of sc to suit your garment, end with a few rows of sc. Fasten off

Flower: Ensure the center opening will fit comfortably over the button and around the buttonhole.
Make the required number of ch, sl st in first ch to form ring.
Round 1: 1 ch, make an even number of sc in the ring (the exact number will be determined by the size of your buttonhole).
Round 2: 3 ch, 1 dc in next sc, *3 ch, 1 dc in each of next 2 sts, rep from * to end, 3 ch, sl st in top of 3 ch. Fasten off.
Sew ring of flower around buttonhole.

STANDARD BUTTONHOLES
Directory view, page 41

Skill level: Intermediate

Cotton Perle   *To fasten with buttons on a garment or to add decoration.*

METHOD

Make a foundation chain of the required length or work row 1 directly into the garment fabric. You may need to adjust the position of the first buttonhole you work to suit your garment.
Row 1: 1 ch, 1 sc in each st to end, turn. Work as many rows of sc as required.
Buttonhole Row: (Based on 9 stitch width) 2 ch, 3 dc, *1 ch, skip 1 sc, 4 dc, rep from * to end.
Final row: work 1 more row of sc, placing 1 sc into each 1-ch loop. Fasten off.

CLOSE BUTTONHOLES
Directory view, page 41

Skill level: Intermediate

 Cotton perle *To fasten with buttons on a garment or to add decoration*

METHOD

Make a foundation chain of the required length, or work row 1 directly into the item to be trimmed with right side facing.
Row 1: 1 ch, 1 sc in each st to end, turn. You may need to adjust the placement of the buttonholes to suit your garment. The sample was worked as stated below and using a contrasting color.
Work as many rows of sc as required.
Buttonhole row: 1 ch, 1 sc, *2 ch, skip 2 sc, 1 sc in next sc, rep from * to end.
Final row: Work 1 more row of sc, placing 2 sc in each 2-ch loop. Fasten off.

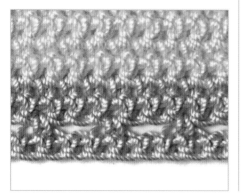

 LOOP BUTTONHOLES
Directory view, page 41

Skill level: Beginner/easy

 Cotton perle *To fasten with buttons on a garment or to add decoration*

METHOD

Make a foundation chain of the required length, or work row 1 directly into the item to be trimmed with right side facing.
Row 1: 1 ch, 1 sc in each st to end, turn. Work as many rows of sc as required.
Place chain loops on the buttonhole row to suit your garment. The sample was worked as stated below and using a contrasting color.
Buttonhole row: 1 ch, 2 sc, *3 ch, 1 sc in each of next 4 sc, rep from * to end. Fasten off.

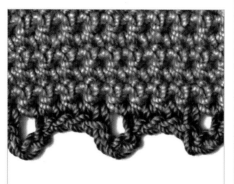

CURVED BUTTONHOLES
Directory view, page 41

Skill level: Intermediate

Cotton perle *To fasten with buttons on a garment or to add decoration*

METHOD

Make a foundation chain of the required length, or work row 1 directly into the item to be trimmed with right side facing.
Before starting decide how many buttonholes are required. Space them evenly over the opening band. To suit your garment, you may need to adjust the number of sc between the 5-ch loops on row 3. The sample was worked with 8 sc between the button holes, giving a multiple of 9 stitches.
Row 1: 1 ch, 1 sc in each st to end, turn.
Row 2: As row 1.
Row 3: 1 ch, 1 sc in first sc, 1 sc in each of next 3 sc, *5 ch, skip 1 sc, 1 sc in each of next 8 sc, rep from * to end, ending last rep with 4 sc, turn.
Row 4: 1 ch, 1 sc in first sc, 1 sc in next sc, *skip 2 sc, (2 ch, 1 dc in 5-ch loop) 4 times, 2 ch, skip 2 sc, 1 sc in each of next 4 sc, rep from * ending last rep with 2 sc. Fasten off.

135 LOOPED PICOT BUTTONHOLES

Directory view, page 42

Skill level: Intermediate

 Cotton perle   *An attractive buttonhole detail*

METHOD

Notes: Picot = 3 ch, I sc in Ist ch.
Before starting decide how many buttonholes are required. Space them evenly over the opening band. To suit your garment, you may need to adjust the number of sc between the 9-ch loops on row 4. The edging is shown in green in the photograph.
Make a foundation chain of the required length, or work row I directly into the item to be trimmed with right side facing.
(multiple of 8 stitches + 5)
Row I: I ch, I sc in each st to end, turn.
Row 2: As row I.
Row 3: As row I.
Row 4: I ch, skip Ist sc, I sc in each of next 4 sc, *9 ch, skip 3 sc, I sc in each of next 5 sc, rep from * to end, turn.
Row 5: I ch, skip Ist sc, I sc in each of next 3 sc, *5 ch, I sc in 9-ch loop, picot, I sc in 9-ch loop, 5 ch, skip I sc, I sc in each of next 3 sc, rep from * to last st, I sc. Fasten off.

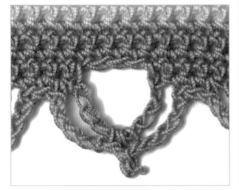

136 PICOT BUTTONHOLES

Directory view, page 42

Skill level: Intermediate

Cotton perle   *To fasten with buttons on a garment or to add decoration*

METHOD

Notes: Picot = 3 ch, sl st into 3rd ch from hook.
Make a foundation chain of the required length, or work row I directly into the item to be trimmed with right side facing.
Row I: I ch, I sc in each st to end, turn.
Work as many rows of sc as required.
Place chain loops on the buttonhole row to suit your garment.
Buttonhole row I: I ch, 2 sc, *3 ch, skip 3 sc, 4 sc, rep from * to end.
Next row: Work in sc, with 3 sc in each chain loop.
Final row: I ch, *sc to center sc of next buttonhole, I picot, rep from * to end.
Fasten off.

137 TEXTURED RUFFLE

Directory view, page 42

Skill level: Challenging/complex

Cotton perle   *This is such a dense and textured piece of crochet it will give decorative contrast to any garment*

METHOD

This is formed by working many double crochets into a small space on a background fabric of double crochet to give a fluted effect.
Make a foundation chain of the required length.
Row I: I tr in 5th ch from hook, I tr into each ch to end, turn.
Row 2: 4 ch, I tr into each st to end, DO NOT TURN.
Row 3: 3 ch, work 6 dc down stem of first tr, I dc into st at base of this st, *7 dc up stem of next tr in row, I dc into top of this st, 7 dc down stem of next tr in row, I dc into st at base of this tr, rep from * to end of row.
Fasten off.
Repeat row 3 on the first row that was worked.

DIAMONDS INSERTION
Directory view, page 42

Skill level: Intermediate

 Cotton perle — *An insertion or link allowing two pieces of fabric to be joined together to lengthen a skirt or sleeves*

METHOD

To make one diamond:
Row 1: 5 ch, sl st in first ch to form a ring, 1 ch, 1 sc in ring, 3 ch, 1 hdc in ring, turn.
Row 2: 5 ch, 1 sc in first 3-ch loop, 3 ch (1 sc, 3 ch, 1 hdc) in last 3-ch loop, turn.
Row 3: 5 ch, 1 sc in first 3-ch loop, (3 ch, 1 dc in next 3-ch loop) to last 3-ch loop, (3 ch, 1 sc, 3 ch, 1 hdc) in last 3-ch loop, turn.
Rep row 3 until the diamond is the required size.
Next row: 3 ch, skip first 3-ch loop, 1 sc in next 3-ch loop (3 ch, 1 sc in next 3-ch loop) to last 3-ch loop, turn.
Rep this row the same number of times row 3 was repeated.
Final row: 3 ch, skip next 3-ch loop, 1 hdc into last ch sp. Fasten off.

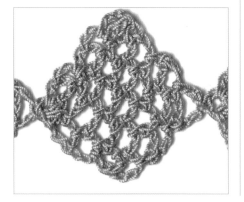

---

139 **DECORATIVE CUFF**
Directory view, page 43

Skill level: Challenging/complex

Cotton perle — *Lengthen a sleeve with this decorative cuff*

METHOD

Notes: dc2tog = work 1 dc in each of next 2 dc until 1 loop of each remains on hook, yo and draw through all 3 loops on hook.
Main section:
Make a foundation chain of the required length, or work row 1 directly into the item to be trimmed with right side facing. (multiple of 4 stitches + 3)
Row 1: 2 ch, *dc2tog over next 2 sts, 1 ch, rep from * to last 2 sts, dc2tog, turn.
Row 2: 3 ch, *dc2tog in next 1-ch loop, 1 ch, rep from * to last 2 sts, dc2tog, turn.
Rep row 2 to the desired length. Do not fasten off, continue with frill section.

Frill section:
Row 1: *5 ch, sl st in top of next dc2tog, rep from * to end, turn.
Row 2: 3 ch, (2 dc, 3 ch, 3 dc) in first 5-ch loop, *2 ch, sl st in next 5-ch loop, 2 ch, 3 dc, 3 ch, 3 dc in next 5-ch loop, rep from * to end, turn.
Row 3: 1 ch, *1 sc in each st to next 3-ch loop, 5 sc in 3-ch loop, rep from * to last 3 sts, 3 sc, turn.
Row 4: 3 ch, 1 dc in each of next 4 sc, *2 dc in each of next 3 sc, 1 dc in each of next 13 sc, rep from * ending last rep with 1 dc in each of next 3 sc, 1 dc in the top of the turning ch. Fasten off.

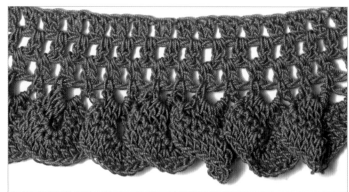

140 # COLUMNS INSERTION
Directory view, page 43

Skill level: Beginner/easy

Cotton perle

An insertion or link allowing two pieces of fabric to be joined together to lengthen a skirt or sleeves

METHOD

Make a foundation chain of the required length or work row 1 directly into the item to be trimmed with right side facing.
(any number of stitches)
Row 1: 1 ch, 1 sc in each ch to end, turn.
Row 2: 4 ch, 1 tr in each sc to end.
Row 3: As row 1.

---

 141 # SPIKED COLUMNS INSERTION
Directory view, page 43

Skill level: Intermediate

Cotton perle in two colors

An insertion or link allowing two pieces of fabric to be joined together to lengthen a skirt or sleeves

METHOD

Notes: There is no right or wrong side, it depends which looks best on the garment. Make a ch of the required length or work row 1 directly into the item to be trimmed.
(any number of stitches)
Row 1: 1 ch, 1 sc in each ch to end, turn.
Row 2: 2 ch, 1 tr in each sc to end.
Row 3: As row 1. Fasten off.
With a contrasting yarn and a larger hook, work loose sl sts along the center of row 2, as shown in the picture. Fasten off.

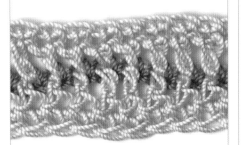

---

 142 # MINI CIRCLES INSERTION
Directory view, page 43

Skill level: Beginner/easy

Cotton perle

To either add texture and interest or to use as an insertion or link allowing two pieces of fabric to be joined together to lengthen a skirt or sleeves

METHOD

Make 5 ch, sl st in first ch to form a ring.
Row 1: 1 ch, 8 sc in ring, sl st in first sc, turn.
Row 2: 1 ch, 2 sc in each sc, sl st in first sc.
Fasten off.

143 BASIC COLLAR
Directory view, page 44

Skill level: Intermediate

Cotton perle | To add interest to any garment neckline or a cushion

METHOD

Make a foundation chain of the required length, or work row 1 directly into the item to be trimmed with right side facing. (multiple of 3 stitches)
Row 1: 1 ch, 1 sc in each st to end, turn.
Row 2: As row 1.
Row 3: 2 ch, 1 dc in each sc to end, turn.
Row 4: 2 ch, *(1 dc, 1 tr, 1 dc) in next dc, 2 dc, rep from * to end, omitting 1 dc at end of last rep, turn.
Row 5: *3 ch, 1 sc in next tr, rep from * to end, ending with 2 ch, sc in last st. Fasten off.

 144 LACE COLLAR
Directory view, page 44

Skill level: Challenging/complex

Cotton perle | To add some interest to any garment neckline or to a cushion

METHOD

Notes: dc2tog = work 1 dc into each of next 2 dc until 1 loop of each remains on hook, yo and draw through all 3 loops on hook. Make a foundation chain of the required length, or work row 1 directly into the item to be trimmed with right side facing. (multiple of 9 stitches + 4)
Row 1: 1 ch, 1 sc in each st to end, turn.
Row 2: 1 ch, 1 sc in first sc, 2 ch, skip 2 sc, 1 sc in next sc, *skip 2 sc, 6 dc in next sc, skip 2 sc, 1 sc in next sc, 2 ch, skip 2 sc, 1 sc in next sc, rep from * to end, turn

Row 3: 1 ch, 1 sc in first sc, 2 ch, *1 dc in next dc, 1 ch, 1 dc in next dc 5 times, 1 sc in next 2 ch sp, rep from * to last 3 sts, omitting 1 sc at end of last rep, 2 ch, 1 sc in last sc.
Row 4: 3 ch, (1 dc in next dc, 2 ch) 4 times, *dc2tog, 2 ch, (1 dc in next dc, 2 ch) 4 times, rep from * to last dc, dc2tog over next dc and sc at end of row. Fasten off.

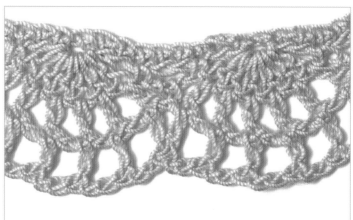

145 INTRICATE LACE COLLAR

Directory view, page 44

Skill level: Challenging/complex

Cotton perle   To add some interest to
any garment neckline or to
a cushion

METHOD

Make a foundation chain of the required length, or work row 1 directly into the item to be trimmed with right side facing. (multiple of 11 stitches)
Row 1: 1 ch, 1 sc in each st to end, turn.
Row 2: 5 ch, 1 dc in 4th sc, *2 ch, skip 1 sc, 1 dc in next sc, rep from * to end, turn.
Row 3: 3 ch, *1 dc in next 2-ch loop, 2 ch, rep from * to last 2-ch loop, 1 dc in loop, 1 dc in top of turning chain, turn.
Row 4: 5 ch, *1 dc in next 2-ch loop, 2 ch, rep from * to end, 1 dc in top of turning ch, turn.

Row 5: 1 ch, 1 sc in first st, 1 sc in next 2-ch loop, *5 ch, 1 sc in next 2-ch loop, 1 sc in next dc, 11 ch, 1 tr in 8th ch from hook, 1 tr in next 2 ch, 1 tr in last sc worked into, skip next 2-ch loop, 1 sc in next dc, 1 sc in next ch loop, 5 ch, 1 sc in next dc, rep from * to last 2-ch loop, 2 sc in loop, turn.
Row 6: 5 ch, *10 sc in next 7-ch loop, 5 ch, 1 sc in 5-ch loop, 1 sc in next 5-ch loop, rep from * to end, working final sc in last st. Fasten off.

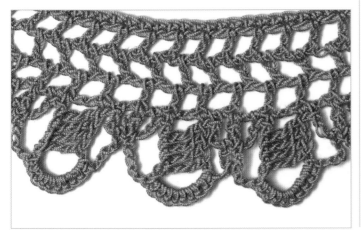

146 FAN COLLAR

Directory view, page 44

Skill level: Beginner/easy

Cotton perle   To add some interest to any garment neckline or to a cushion

METHOD

Main section:
Make a foundation chain of 7 stitches, turn.
Row 1: 3 dc in 6th ch from hook, 2 ch, 3 dc in next ch, turn.
Row 2: 5 ch, (3 dc, 2 ch, 3 dc) in 2-ch loop, *1 dc in top of turning ch, turn.
Row 3: 3 ch, (3 dc, 2 ch, 3dc) in 2-ch sp, turn.
Rep rows 2 and 3 until straight edge fits around neck, ending on row 2, work last repeat of row 2 to *, 2 ch, 1 dc in 2-ch loop at end of previous row. Fasten off.

Inner edging:
Position collar so shells point toward the center front, rejoin yarn to straight edge: 1 ch, 2 dc into each sp along edge. Fasten off.
Outer edging:
On RS rejoin yarn into 5-ch loop at edge of collar, 3 ch, 8 dc in same loop, 9 dc in each 5-ch loop to end, work 1 dc in the 2-ch loop or between 3 dc groups at end of last row of main section of collar. Fasten off.

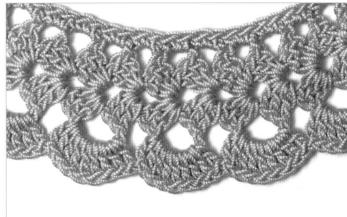

147 PICOT COLLAR

Directory view, page 44

Skill level: Beginner/easy

Cotton perle

To add an attractive collar to a garment neckline

METHOD

Make a foundation chain of the required length, or work row 1 directly into the item to be trimmed with right side facing. (multiple of 7 stitches)

Row 1: 1 ch, 1 sc in 2nd ch from hook, 1 sc in each of next 5 ch, *turn, 7 ch, skip 5 sc, 1 sc in next sc, turn, (6 sc, 5 ch, 6 sc) in 7-ch loop, 1 sc in next 6 foundation ch, rep from * to end, omitting 6 sc at end of last rep.

148 RINGS BELT

Directory view, page 45

Skill level: Beginner/easy

Cotton perle

To make an attractive and unusual belt

5 circular craft rings
A length of fine braid to link the covered rings together

METHOD

The belt shown uses five rings in leaf green. Each ring is covered in the same way. Make a slip knot in the usual way and work sc into a plastic craft ring as if you were working into a chain ring: covering the ring completely. Ensure that the stitches are pushed closely together to fully cover the ring when the belt is worn. Fasten off and sew in all the yarn ends.

Place the rings in three layers as shown in the photograph and weave the braid through them. You may make more groups to use around the belt.

Secure the ends of the braid with a few stitches.

149 DOUBLE RINGS BELT
Directory view, page 45

Skill level: Beginner/easy

Cotton perle in two contrasting shades

7 circular craft rings
A length of fine decorative braid to link the covered rings together

To make an attractive and unusual belt

METHOD

The belt shown uses four rings in jade green and three rings in sage green. Each ring is covered in the same way.

Make a slip knot in the usual way and work sc into a plastic craft ring as if you were working into a chain ring: covering the ring completely. Ensure that the stitches are pushed closely together to fully cover the ring when the belt is worn. Fasten off and sew in all the yarn ends.

Place the rings in two layers as shown in the photograph and weave the braid through them. You may make more groups of covered rings to use around the belt. Secure the ends of the braid with a few stitches.

150 BEADED BELT TIE
Directory view, page 45

Skill level: Beginner/easy

Cotton perle in two colors: A and B.

5 mm glass seed beads

To add decoration to a belt

METHOD

Make an sc belt 2–4 inches (5–10 cm) wide and to the required length. This can be worked as a few rows of the required length or as a large number of rows of required depth. You may need to make more lengths of chain for the tie if your belt is wider than the 2-inch (5-cm) width shown.

Tie detail : Decide on the finished length of tie. For each end of the belt, make 2 lengths of chain in the yarn used to make the belt (yarn A) and 4 lengths in a contrasting color (yarn B).

Arrange the chains in the following order: B A B B A B, fold in two and sew in place, using the picture as a guide.

Slide 3 beads onto each length of chain and tie a small knot at the end to secure beads in place. Tie a second knot at the top of these beads. Sew in the yarn ends.

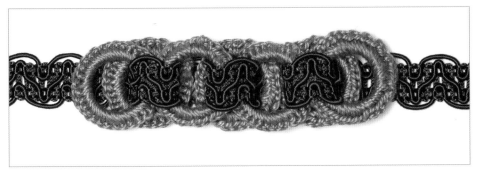

PROJECTS

The five projects in this chapter are designed to provide ideas and inspiration for using the trims in the directory. As well as looking at how the trims can be applied to existing garments and soft furnishings the projects also demonstrate how varying the yarns and beads used in the directory can bring a whole new look to the trims.

BOBBLE BOLERO

This classic pink bolero for a little girl has been made into a party piece by attaching dangling ball buttons to the hem and as a button. The crochet on these hanging buttons is chunky and fun. The buttons have been filled with batting to give greater volume and interest without adding weight. A bright orange trim has also been added to the garment edge.

GARMENT EDGE

Starting at the left-hand edge opposite the buttonhole with right side of garment facing, work 1 row of sl st in orange around the lower edge of the ribbing—147 ch. Work 23 ch around the button hole to form a circle about ³⁄₁₆ inch (5 mm) out from the buttonhole edge. Fasten off. You may need to adjust the number of stitches around the hem of the bolero to suit the garment you are working on.

WORKING THE BALL BUTTON

Using the pattern for the Ball button (trim 128), make seven buttons in pink and seven in orange. You will also need to make a slightly smaller pink button for the buttonhole.

Note: The covering for this type of button should be made a little small and the button should be firmly stuffed with washable batting or yarn.

Make 2 ch.
Round 1: 6 sc in 2nd ch from hook, sl st in first sc.
Round 2: 1 ch, 2 sc in each sc, sl st in first sc.
Round 3: 1 ch, 1 sc in each sc, sl st in first sc. (This completes the first half of this spherical button. Sew in the loose yarn at the beginning of round 1).
Round 4: 1 ch, (1 sc, skip 1 sc) 6 times, sl st in first sc.
Insert some yarn or washable batting into the center to pack out the button.
Round 5: 1 ch, (1 sc, skip 1 sc) 3 times, sl st in first sc.

Fasten off leaving at least 4 inches (10 cm) of yarn to close the base of the button (after stuffing) and attach it to the garment.

FINISHING

Make three evenly spaced knots of the length of yarn left on the buttons. With a yarn needle sew the buttons to the orange sl st row on the jacket at regular intervals, alternating the colors.

TRY THIS

You could try using a fine yarn to make clusters of two or three hanging bobbles or you could try arranging some more bobbles around the body of the cardigan.

PROJECT 2

Skill level: Intermediate

Trim used: 28 Posy Edge

YOU WILL NEED

- Wrap-around cardigan
- Yarn: Fingering weight merino/cashmere mixture in co-ordinating colors, here spring green is used
- Size E (3.5 mm) crochet hook

POSY-EDGED CARDIGAN

This lightweight wrap-around cardigan has been greatly enhanced by the posy edge, which has been hand-sewn to the neckline and to the sleeve edges. Worked in a soft and delicate fingering-weight, merino/cashmere yarn, this intricate edging creates a refreshing and elegant effect.

WORKING THE POSY EDGE

Using the pattern for trim 28, Posy Edge, work the following:
A length of 22 motifs for neck edge—length 28 inches (72 cm).
A length of 10 motifs for each of the sleeve edges—length 12 inches (31 cm).

Note: You may need to adjust the number of motifs if the size of your garment is different to the one shown in the picture. As there is no foundation chain for this edging, this is very easy to achieve.

There is no foundation chain for this edging.
Row 1: 4 ch, 1 dc in 4th ch from hook (center ring made), (3 ch, 2 dc into ring, 3 ch, 1 sl st in ring) 3 times (3 petals made = 1 motif), *11 ch, 1 dc into 4th ch from hook, 3 ch, 1 dc in ring, 1 sl st between 2 dc of last petal made, 1 dc into ring, 3 ch, 1 sl st in ring, (3 ch, 2 dc in ring, 3 ch, 1 sl st in ring) twice, rep from * to length required. Fasten off.

PATTERN VARIATION

To finish the tapering neckline, rejoin yarn to each end in turn, 1 dc, 2 sc. Fasten off.

FINISHING

Pin the edgings into position and hand sew with a matching thread using back stitch or any basic, small, neat stitch.

TRY THIS

To achieve a formal evening look you could try using a silky yarn in deep green for the posy trim. You could also stitch beads around the center of the posies.

PROJECT 3

Skill level: Complex/challenging

Trims used: 45 Curlicue fringe
124 Snowflake

YOU WILL NEED

- Silk pillow cover, 18 x 18 inches
  (45 x 45 cm)

- Yarn A: Sport weight wool/cotton
  mixture in a co-ordinating color, here
  burnt orange

- Yarn B: Fingering weight wool/nylon
  mixture in co-ordinating variegated
  shades, here autumnal shades are used

- Size C (3 mm) crochet hook

FRILLED PILLOW

This rich mixture of autumnal shades lends a special texture to a plain orange pillow cover. The fringe is worked with random spacing between the curlicues, allowing for a certain amount of personal creativity in the project, it also allows for any variation in the lengths of the pillow edges. The motif, on the other hand, provides a contrast with its uniform and structured appearance.

WORKING THE CURLICUE FRINGE

First section
Using yarn A, (leave a long end, in case you need to adjust the length) make a length of chain to fit just inside the edge of the pillow cover, plus twelve chains.
(multiple of 4 stitches + 1)
1 sc in 2nd ch, *1 sc in each ch to the next corner of the pillow cover, skip 3 ch, rep from * to end, fasten off. Do not join the ends of the strip together at this stage, it will be easier to work the second section.

Second section
Use yarn B to complete the fringe.
Row 1: Join yarn to the opposite side of the foundation chain, with the same side of the work facing as for the first section, work one row of sc, including working 1 sc in each of the ch skipped on the first section, turn.
Row 2: 2 ch, *1 hdc in each st to the next corner, 3 hdc in center of corner, rep from * to end, turn.
Row 3: As row 2.

Row 4: 1 ch, *3 sc (see pattern variation below), ^9 ch, 4 sc in 3rd ch from hook, (4 dc in next ch) 6 times, 1 sl st in last sc worked on fringe header ^, rep from ^ to ^ once, rep from * to end. Fasten off.

PATTERN VARIATION

Row 4: 3, 4, or 5 sc were randomly worked between each curlicue to provide a relaxed and laid back appearance.

Corner details: work one curlicue 2 or 3 sts either side of each corner and one curlicue directly on the corner.

Note: Leave the ends of yarn at the beginning and the end of this fringe, as they can be used to weave the two edges together after the fringe has been sewn onto the pillow cover.

WORKING THE SNOWFLAKE

Using Yarn A, and the size C (3 mm) crochet hook make 8 ch, sl st in first ch to form a ring.

Round 1: 2 ch, 17 hdc in ring, join in top of 2 ch at beg of round.

Round 2: 1 ch, 1 sc in same st, *17 ch, 1 sc in each of next 3 sts, rep from * 5 times, ending last rep with sc in next 2 sts, sl st in first sc.

Round 3: 1 ch, 1 sc in same st, *23 sc in next 17-ch loop, 1 sc in each of next 2 sc, 7 ch, sl st in same sc, 1 sc in next sc, rep from * 5 times, ending last rep with 7 ch, sl st in same dc, sl st in first sc. Fasten off.

FINISHING

Attach the fringe and motif to the pillow cover by pinning into position and then hand-sewing with a matching thread using back stitch or any small, neat stitch. Join the ends of the fringe and fasten off all ends.

TRY THIS

An alternative way to work the fringing on this cushion is to have double or triple rows of fringing worked in contrasting textures and colors.

DOUBLE-TRIMMED SKIRT

Adding two different crochet braids to this basic white skirt adds interest and texture to a plain garment. Position the braids so that there is a gap between them suitable to allow them to interact visually.

PROJECT 4

Skill level: Intermediate

Trims used: 76 Jazzy braid (top)
              86 Angled chevrons (bottom)

YOU WILL NEED

- Basic white cotton skirt

- Fingering weight merino/cashmere mixture yarn in a complementary color, here spring green is used

- 67 5 mm matte glass beads (25 beads for the upper trim and 42 for the lower trim) in a color complementary or toning to the yarn, here pink is used

- Size E (3.5 mm) crochet hook

FINISHED SIZE

Trim 76, Jazzy braid, the upper trim, is 45 inches (114 cm) long.
Trim 86, Angled chevrons, the lower trim, is 47 inches (120 cm) long.

WORKING THE UPPER TRIM (JAZZY BRAID)

Thread 25 beads onto the yarn before starting work.
Make a foundation chain of the required length.
(multiple of 10 stitches + 1)
Row 1: 1 sc in 2nd ch from hook, 1 sc in each ch to end, turn.
Row 2: 1 ch, working along the opposite side of the foundation chain, *bring down a bead to work into next sc, 9 sc, rep from * to end. Fasten off.

WORKING THE LOWER TRIM (ANGLED CHEVRONS)

Thread 42 beads onto the yarn before starting work.
Make a foundation chain of the required length.
(multiple of 14 stitches + 2)
Row 1: 1 ch, 2 sc in second ch from hook, *1 sc in each of next 8 ch, skip 1 ch, 1 sc in each of next 4 ch, 3 dc in next ch, rep from * to end, omitting 1 sc at end of last rep, turn.
Row 2: 1 ch, 2 sc in first sc, *1 sc into each of next 3 sc, bring down 1 bead to work into next sc, skip 1 sc, bring down 1 bead to work into next sc, 1 sc in each of next 8 sc, 3 sc in next ch, rep from * to last long section of chevron, end with 2 sc in last st. Fasten off.

FINISHING

Pin the trims into position and hand-sew with a matching thread using back stitch or any basic small, neat stitch.

TRY THIS

If you wanted to trim a winter skirt you could try using a chunkier DK yarn with larger beads. Alternatively, you could try making one or two more additional trims to add interest and texture.

PROJECT 5

Skill level: Beginner/easy

Trim used: 123 Pearl rose
98 Irish leaf

YOU WILL NEED

- Beret

- Sport weight cotton yarn in a complementary color, here pink and burnt orange are used

- 5 1 cm heart-shaped pearl beads in a co-ordinating color for the center of the rose, here pink beads are used

- Size E (3.5 mm) crochet hook

EMBELLISHED BERET

These charming motifs are simple, quick, and fun to make and they are great for embellishing any item of clothing. The large two-colored flower and Irish leaf used in this project add a bold, fun detail to this beret.

WORKING THE IRISH LEAF

Work the leaf motif in pink with a total of 6 rows.
Note: Work into back loop only on each repeat of row 2.
Make 11 ch.
Row 1: Working into one loop only along first side of ch, 1 sc in 2nd ch from hook, 1 sc in each of next 8 ch, 3 sc in last ch, working in one loop only along other side of foundation ch, 1 sc into each of next 7 ch, turn.
Row 2: Working in back loop only, 1 ch, 1 sc in first sc, 1 sc in each of next 7 sc, 3 sc in next sc, 1 sc in each of next 7 sc, turn.
Rep row 2 as many times as desired. Fasten off.

WORKING THE PEARL ROSE

Notes: Work rounds 1–3 in pink, rounds 4–7 in burnt orange, and rounds 8–9 in pink.
Make 6 ch, sl st in 1 ch to form a ring.
Round 1: 1 ch, 17 sc in ring, sl st in first ch.
Round 2: 5 ch, skip next 2 sc, *1 sc in next sc, 4 ch, skip next 2 sc, rep from * to end, sl st in 2nd of 5 ch at beg of round.
Round 3: *(1 sc, 1 hdc, 5 dc, 1 hdc, 1 sc) in next 4-ch loop, rep from * to end, sl st in first sc.

Round 4: *5 ch, pass these ch behind next group of sts, 1 sc in next sc of round 2, inserting the hook from behind, rep from * to end.
Round 5: *(1 sc, 1 hdc, 10 dc, 1 hdc, 1 sc) in next 5-ch loop, rep from * to end, sl st in first sc.
Round 6: *7 ch, pass these ch behind next group of sts, 1 sc in next sc of round 4, inserting the hook from behind, rep from * to end.
Round 7: *(1 sc, 1 hdc, 15 dc, 1 hdc, 1 sc) in next 7-ch loop, rep from * to end, sl st in first sc.
Round 8: *8 ch, pass these ch behind next group of sts, 1 sc in next sc of 6th round inserting the hook from behind, rep from * to end.
Round 9: *(1 sc, 1 hdc, 5 dc, 10 tr, 5 dc, 1 hdc, 1 sc) in next 7-ch loop, rep from * to end, sl st in first sc. Fasten off.
Making up: Arrange and sew the heart shaped pearl beads in the center of the flower.

FINISHING

Pin the motifs into position on the beret and hand-sew with a matching thread using back stitch or any basic small, neat stitch.

For a different effect, try using a fine yarn for the center rounds of the motif and a thicker, chunkier yarn for the outer two rounds.

REFRESHER COURSE

This Refresher Course in crochet skills will guide you through everything you need to make all of the trims in this book. Information is supplied on all the fundamentals from choosing hook and yarn and working basic stitches, to working textured stitches, working in the round, and adding beads and sequins.

MATERIALS AND EQUIPMENT

Crochet is one of the easiest crafts to take up because you need very little initial equipment: just a ball of yarn and a crochet hook. Other accessories, such as pins and sharp scissors, are useful and relatively inexpensive.

YARNS

There are a huge range of yarns available to use for crochet, from very fine cotton to chunky wool. Yarns can be made from one fiber or combine a mixture of two or three different ones. As a general rule, the easiest yarns to use for crochet have a smooth surface and a medium or tight twist.

Woolen yarns and blended yarns with a high proportion of wool feel good to crochet with as they have a certain amount of stretch, making it easy to push the point of the hook into each stitch. Silk yarn has a delightful luster, but it has less resilience than either wool or cotton and is much more expensive. Yarns made from cotton and linen are durable and cool to wear, and may be blended with other fibers to add softness. Yarns made wholly from synthetic fibers, such as acrylic or nylon, are usually less expensive to buy than those made from natural fibers, but can pill when worn and lose their shape. A good solution is to choose a yarn with a small proportion of synthetic fibers that has been combined with a natural fiber, such as wool or cotton.

Yarn is sold by weight, rather than by length, although the packaging of many yarns now includes the length per ball as well as the weight.

HOOKS

Crochet hooks are available in a wide range of sizes, shapes, and materials. The most common sorts of hooks are made from aluminum or plastic. Small sizes of steel hooks are also made for working crochet with very fine cotton yarns. Hand-made wooden, bamboo, and horn hooks are also available, many featuring decorative handles.

There appears to be no standardization of hook sizing between manufacturers. The points and throats of different brands of hooks often vary in shape which affects the size of stitch they produce.

Hook sizes are quoted differently in the United States and Europe and some brands of hooks are labeled with more than one type of numbering. Choosing a hook is largely a matter of personal preference.

The hook sizes quoted in pattern instructions are a very useful guide, but you may find that you need to use smaller or larger hook sizes, depending on the brand, to achieve the correct gauge for a pattern. The most important thing to consider when choosing a hook is how it feels in your hand and the ease with which it works with your yarn. When you have found your perfect brand of hook, it's useful to buy a range of several different sizes.

USEFUL HOOK/YARN COMBINATIONS

Sport weight (4ply) B–E
(2.5–3.5 mm)
Double knitting (DK) E–G
(3.5–4.5 mm)
Worsted weight (Aran) I–J
(5–6 mm)

US/METRIC EQUIVALENTS

1 oz = 28 g
2 oz = 57 g
1¾ oz = 50 g
3½ oz = 100 g
1 inch = 2.5 cm
4 inches = 10 cm
1 yard = 91.4 cm
39½ inches = 1 m

YARN TYPES AND WEIGHTS

Yarns are available in a range of weights varying from very fine to very bulky. Although each weight of yarn is described by a specific name, as shown in the samples below, there may actually be a lot of variation in the thicknesses when yarns are produced by different manufacturers or in different countries.

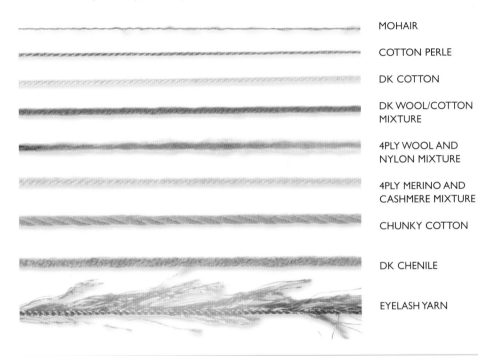

MOHAIR

COTTON PERLE

DK COTTON

DK WOOL/COTTON MIXTURE

4PLY WOOL AND NYLON MIXTURE

4PLY MERINO AND CASHMERE MIXTURE

CHUNKY COTTON

DK CHENILE

EYELASH YARN

ADDITIONAL EQUIPMENT

TAPE MEASURE
Choose one that shows both inches and centimeters on the same side and replace when it becomes worn or frayed.

MARKERS
Split rings or shaped loops can be used to mark a place on a pattern, to indicate the beginning row of a repeat, and to help with counting the stitches on the foundation chain.

YARN NEEDLES
Yarn needles come in a range of sizes and are used for weaving in yarn ends and for sewing pieces of crochet together.

PINS
Glass-headed pins are the best type to use for blocking. Quilters' long pins with fancy heads are useful when pinning pieces of crochet together as the heads are easy to see and won't slip through the crochet fabric.

ROW COUNTER
A knitter's row counter will help you keep track of the number of rows you have worked, or you may prefer to use a notebook and pencil.

SHARP SCISSORS
Choose a small, pointed pair to cut yarn and trim off yarn ends.

COMPARATIVE CROCHET HOOK SIZES (FROM SMALLEST TO LARGEST)						
STEEL			ALUMINUM OR PLASTIC			
US	UK	METRIC (MM)	US	UK	METRIC (MM)	
14	6	0.60		14	2.00	
13	5½			13		
12	5	0.75	B	12	2.50	
11	4½		C	11	3.00	
10	4	1.00	D	10		
9	3½		E	9	3.50	
8	3	1.25	F	8	4.00	
7	2½	1.50	G	7	4.50	
6	2	1.75	H	6	5.00	
5	1½		I	5	5.50	
4	1	2.00	J	4	6.00	
3	1/0		K	2	7.00	
2	2/0	2.50				
1	3/0	3.00				
0						
00		3.5				

BASIC SKILLS

HOLDING THE HOOK AND YARN

1 Holding the hook as if it was a pen is the most widely used method. Center the tips of your right thumb and forefinger over the flat section of the hook.

2 An alternative way to hold the hook is to grasp the flat section of the hook between your right thumb and forefinger as if you were holding a knife.

3 To control the supply and keep an even tension on the yarn, loop the short end of the yarn over your left forefinger and take the yarn coming from the ball loosely around the little finger on the same hand. Use the middle finger on the same hand to help hold the work. If left-handed, hold the hook in the left hand and the yarn in the right.

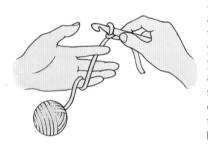

WORKING A FOUNDATION CHAIN(CH)

The foundation chain is the equivalent of casting on in knitting and it's important to make sure that you have made the required number of chains for the pattern you are going to work. Count each V-shaped loop on the front of the chain as one chain stitch, except for the loop on the hook which is not counted. You may find it easier to turn the chain over and count the stitches on the back of the chain. When working the first row of stitches (usually called the foundation row) into the chain, insert the hook under two threads in most instances.

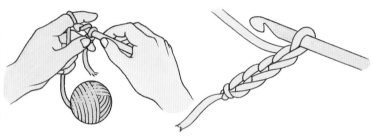

1 Holding the hook with the slip knot and the yarn in your left hand, wrap the yarn over the hook. Draw the yarn through to make a new loop and complete the first chain stitch.

2 Repeat this step, drawing a new loop of yarn through the loop already on the hook until the chain is the required length. Move the thumb and middle finger that are grasping the chain upward after every few stitches to keep the tension even. When working into the chain, insert the hook under two threads for a firm edge, unless otherwise indicated in your pattern.

MAKING A SLIP KNOT

1 Loop the yarn as shown, insert the hook into the loop, catch the yarn with the hook and pull it through to make a loop over the hook.

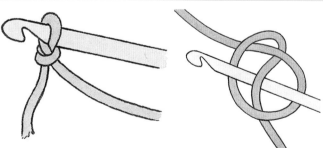

2 Gently pull the yarn to tighten the loop around the hook and complete the slip knot.

ALTERNATIVE SLIP KNOT

To work a number of stitches into a slip knot, you may need to make the slip knot so that it slides up from the ball end of the yarn rather than the tail. To do this, place the yarn ball at the left and the tail at the right as shown in the diagram, left.

TURNING CHAINS

When working crochet in rows or rounds, you will need to work a specific number of extra chains at the beginning of each row or round. The extra chains are needed to bring the hook up to the correct height for the particular stitch you will be working next. When the work is turned at the end of a straight row, the extra chains are called a turning chain, and when they are worked at the beginning of a round, they are called a starting chain.

The turning or starting chain is usually counted as the first stitch of the row, except when working single crochet where the single turning chain is ignored. For example, *ch 3 (counts as 1 dc)* at the beginning of a row or round means that the turning or starting chain contains three chain stitches and these are counted as the equivalent of one double crochet stitch. A chain may be longer than the number required for the stitch and in that case, counts as one stitch plus a number of chains. For example, *ch 5 (counts as 1 dc, ch 2)* means that the chain is the equivalent of one double crochet stitch plus two chain stitches.

At the end of the row or round, the final stitch is usually worked into the turning or starting chain worked on the previous row or round. The final stitch may be worked into the top chain of the turning or starting chain or into another specified stitch of the chain. For example, *1 dc into 3rd of ch 5* means that the final stitch is a double crochet stitch and is worked into the 3rd stitch of the turning or starting chain.

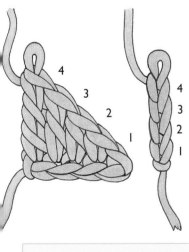

The box below shows the correct number of chain stitches needed to make a turn for each stitch.

SINGLE CROCHET STITCH (SC) - 1 chain to turn

HALF DOUBLE CROCHET STITCH (HDC) - 2 chains to turn

DOUBLE CROCHET STITCH (DC) - 3 chains to turn

TREBLE CROCHET STITCH (TR) - 4 chains to turn

STITCHES

WORKING A SLIP STITCH

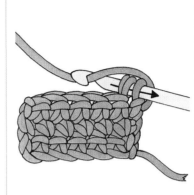

Slip stitch is the shortest of all the crochet stitches and its main uses are for joining rounds, making seams, and carrying the hook and yarn from one place to another. Insert the hook from front to back into the required stitch. Wrap the yarn over the hook (yarn over) and draw it through both the work and the loop on the hook. One loop remains on the hook and one slip stitch has been worked.

WORKING A SINGLE CROCHET

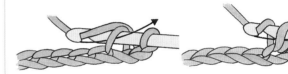

1 Begin with a foundation chain and insert the hook from front to back into the second chain from the hook. Wrap the yarn over the hook (yarn over) and draw it through the first loop, leaving two loops on the hook.

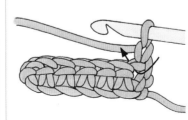

2 To complete the stitch, yarn over and draw it through both loops on the hook, leaving one loop on the hook. Continue in this way, working one single crochet into each chain.

3 At the end of the row, turn, work one chain for the turning chain (remember that this chain does not count as a stitch). Insert the hook into the first single crochet at the beginning of the row. Work a single crochet into each stitch of the previous row, being careful to work the final stitch into the last stitch of the row, but not into the turning chain.

WORKING A HALF DOUBLE CROCHET

1 Begin with a foundation chain, wrap the yarn over the hook (yarn over) and insert the hook into the third chain from the hook.

2 Draw the yarn through the chain, leaving three loops on the hook. Yarn over and draw through all three loops on the hook, leaving one loop on the hook. One half double stitch complete.

3 Continue along the row, working one half double crochet into each chain. At the end of the row, work two chains to turn. Skip the first stitch and work a half double crochet into each stitch made on the previous row. At the end of the row, work the last stitch into the top of the turning chain.

WORKING A DOUBLE CROCHET

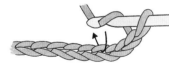 

1 Begin with a foundation chain, wrap the yarn over the hook and insert the hook into the fourth chain from the hook.

2 Draw the yarn through the chain, leaving three loops on the hook. Yarn over again and draw the yarn through the first two loops on the hook, leaving two loops on the hook.

3 Yarn over and draw the yarn through the two loops on the hook leaving one loop on the hook. One double crochet complete. Continue along the row, working one double crochet stitch into each chain. At the end of the row, work three chains to turn. Skip the first stitch and work a double crochet into each stitch made on the previous row. At the end of the row, work the last stitch into the top of the turning chain.

WORKING A TREBLE CROCHET

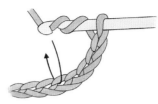 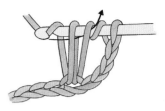

1 Begin with a foundation chain, wrap the yarn over the hook twice (yarn over twice) and insert the hook into the fifth chain from the hook.

2 Draw the yarn through the chain, leaving four loops on the hook. Yarn over again and draw the yarn through the first two loops on the hook, leaving three loops on the hook.

3 Yarn over again and draw through the first two loops on the hook leaving two loops on the hook.

4 Yarn over again and draw through the two remaining loops, leaving one loop on the hook. Treble crochet complete.

5 Continue along the row, working one treble crochet stitch into each chain. At the end of the row, work four chains to turn. Skip the first stitch and work a treble crochet into each stitch made on the previous row. At the end of the row, work the last stitch into the top of the turning chain.

WORKING INTO THE FRONT AND BACK OF STITCHES

Unless pattern details instruct you otherwise, it's usual to work crochet stitches under both loops of the stitches made on the previous row.

WORKING INTO FRONT

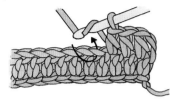

When instructions tell you to work into the front of the stitches, insert the hook only under the front loops of stitches on the previous row.

WORKING INTO BACK

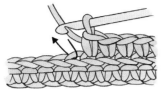

Likewise, to work into the back of the stitches, insert the hook only under the back loops of stitches on the previous row.

JOINING YARNS

Sometimes yarn is fastened off in one position and then rejoined elsewhere (to work an edging, for example). Also, if your first ball of yarn runs out, you will have to join in another. You can also join in a new yarn using the changing colors method.

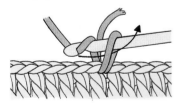

Insert the hook as the pattern requires, wrap the yarn over it, and pull a loop through. Leave a tail of about 4 inches (10 cm). Work one chain, and continue the pattern. If you are using a solid stitch work the next few stitches for about 2 inches (5 cm) enclosing the yarn tail, then pull gently on the tail and snip off the excess.

CHANGING COLORS

1 To make a neat join between colors, leave the last stitch of the old color incomplete so there are two loops on the hook and wrap the new color around the hook.

2 Draw the new color through to complete the stitch and continue working in the new color. The illustrations show a color change in a row of double crochet stitches—the method is the same for single crochet and other stitches.

FASTENING OFF YARN

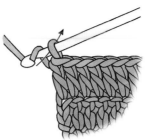

1 To fasten off the yarn at the end of a piece of crochet, cut the yarn 6 inches (15 cm) from the last stitch. Work one chain stitch with the yarn end and pull the yarn end through the chain stitch with the hook.

2 Gently pull the yarn end to tighten the chain stitch and weave the end in on the wrong side of the work (see below).

WEAVING A YARN END ALONG TOP EDGE

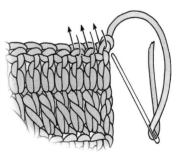

To weave a yarn end in at the top of the work, thread the end in a large yarn needle. Weave the end through several stitches on the wrong side of the work. Trim the remaining yarn.

WEAVING A YARN END ALONG LOWER EDGE

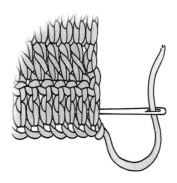

To weave a yarn end in along the lower edge, thread the end in a yarn needle and draw it through several stitches on the wrong side of the work. Trim the remaining yarn.

TEXTURED STITCHES

WORKING PUFF STITCHES

A puff stitch is a cluster of half double stitches worked in the same place—the number of stitches in each puff can vary between three and five. When working a beginning puff stitch, count the turning chain as the first stitch.

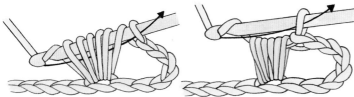

I Wrap the yarn over the hook, insert the hook into the stitch, yarn over hook again and draw a loop through (three loops on the hook). Repeat this step twice more, inserting the hook into the same stitch (seven loops on the hook).

2 Wrap the yarn over the hook and draw it through all seven loops on the hook. Work an extra chain stitch at the top of the puff to complete the stitch.

WORKING BOBBLES

A bobble is a cluster of between three and five double crochet stitches worked into the same stitch and closed at the top. Bobbles are worked on wrong side rows and they are usually surrounded by shorter stitches to throw them into high relief. When working contrasting bobbles, use a separate length of yarn to make each bobble, carrying the main yarn across the back of the bobble.

To make a three stitch bobble, wrap the yarn over the hook, work the first stitch, omitting the last stage to leave two loops on the hook. Work the second and third stitches in the same way. You now have four loops on the hook. Wrap the yarn over the hook and draw it through the four loops to secure them and complete the bobble.

WORKING POPCORNS

A popcorn stitch is a cluster of double crochet stitches (the number may vary), which is folded and closed at the top. When working a beginning popcorn, count the turning chain as the first stitch.

I To make a popcorn with four stitches, work a group of four double crochet stitches into the same place.

2 Take the hook out of the working loop and insert it under both loops of the first double crochet in the group. Pick up the working loop with the hook and draw it through to fold the group of stitches and close it at the top.

WORKING BULLIONS

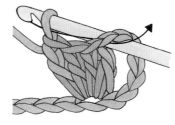

A bullion stitch is formed by wrapping the yarn several times (normally seven to ten) around the hook, and pulling a loop through. Bullions should be worked on right side rows.

I Wrap the yarn (not too tightly) as many times as directed around the hook. Insert the hook where required, and pull through a loop. Wrap the yarn around the hook again.

2 Pull through all the loops on the hook. You can ease each loop in turn off the hook, rather than try to pull through all of them at once.

WORKING AROUND THE POST

This technique creates raised stitches by inserting the hook around the post (stem) of the stitch below, from the front or the back.

FRONT POST DOUBLE CROCHET

Wrap the yarn over the hook from back to front (yo), insert the hook from the front to the back at right of the next stitch, then bring it to the front at the left of the same stitch. Complete the stitch in the usual way.

BACK POST DOUBLE CROCHET

Wrap the yarn over the hook, insert the hook from the back to the front at right of the next stitch, then take it back again at the left of the same stitch. Complete the stitch in the usual way.

WORKING SPIKE STITCHES

Spikes are made by inserting the hook one or more rows below the previous row, either directly below the next stitch or to the right or left.

To work a single crochet spike stitch, insert the hook as directed by the pattern, wrap the yarn over the hook and draw through, lengthening the loop to the height of the working row, then complete the stitch.

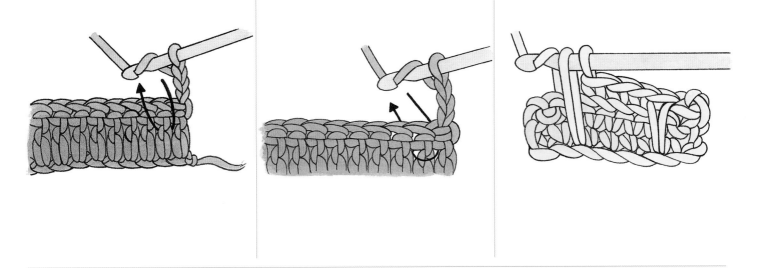

MAKING A FRINGE

You can make a fringe directly into a garment edge or first work one or more rows of single crochet edging around the garment to give a firm edge.

Cut the yarn twice the required length of the fringe plus a little extra length to account for the knot. Take a number of lengths (as stated in the pattern) and fold in half. Insert a large hook through the crochet edge from back to front and draw the folded end of the yarn through to make a loop. Hook the ends through the loop and gently tighten the knot. Repeat at regular intervals along the crochet edge and then trim the ends evenly with sharp scissors.

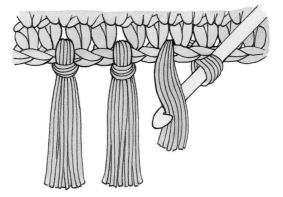

WORKING IN ROUNDS

Motifs worked in rounds are worked outward from a central ring of chains called a foundation ring.

MAKING A FOUNDATION RING

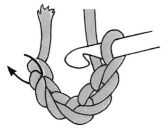

Work a short length of foundation chain (page 114) as specified in the pattern. Join the chains into a ring by working a slip stitch into the first stitch of the foundation chain.

WORKING INTO THE RING

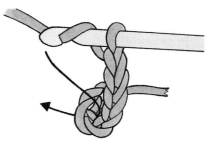

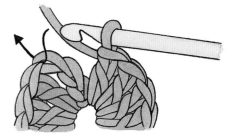

1 Work the number of turning chains specified in the pattern—three chains are shown here (counting as a double crochet stitch). Inserting the hook into the space at the center of the ring each time, work the number of stitches specified in the pattern into the ring. Count the stitches at the end of the round to check you have worked the correct number.

2 Join the first and last stitches of the round together by working a slip stitch into the top of the turning chain.

FINISHING OFF THE FINAL ROUND

To make a neat edge, finish off the final round by using this method of sewing the first and last stitches together in preference to the slip stitch joining method shown above.

1 Cut the yarn, leaving an end of about 4 inches (10cm) and draw it through the last stitch. With right side facing, thread the end in a large yarn needle and take it under both loops of the stitch next to the turning chain.

2 Pull the needle through and insert it into the center of the last stitch of the round. On the wrong side, pull the needle through to complete the stitch, adjust the length of the stitch to close the round, then weave in the end on the wrong side in the usual way.

THREE-DIMENSIONAL MOTIFS

Initially, three-dimensional flower motifs seem a little tricky to work until you get the hang of holding the previously worked petals out of the way so you can work the foundation chains for the next layer directly behind them. This is one of those "practice makes perfect" techniques so don't give up if your first few rows of petals don't look very neat. Try using a size smaller hook to work the chains, then change back to the normal size when making the petals. This makes it easier to insert the hook between the petals when joining the chains.

MAKING CROCHET BUTTONS

Crochet buttons are fun to make, whether ball buttons or flat ring buttons, and they can be made to match or contrast in color with a garment or pillow cover.

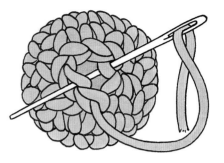

MAKING A BALL BUTTON

1 Work a ball button over a bead or a small ball of stuffing. Using a smaller hook than suggested for the yarn you are using, ch 2, then work 4 sc into the first ch. Without joining or turning the work, work 2 sc into each stitch made on the previous round. For the next and every following increase round, work * 1 sc in first st, 2 sc into next stitch;

repeat from * until the piece covers one half of the bead or ball of stuffing.

2 Slip the bead or ball into the cover. Start decreasing by working * 1 sc into next st, sc2tog; repeat from * until the bead or ball is completely covered.

3 Break off the yarn, leaving an end of about 12 inches (30 cm). Thread the yarn into a large yarn needle and work a few stitches to secure. Don't cut the yarn, instead use it to attach the button to the garment.

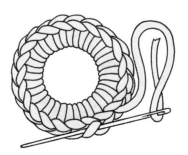

MAKING A RING BUTTON

1 Work a ring button over a plastic ring—choose a ring which is slightly smaller than the size you require for the finished button. Starting with a slip knot on the hook, work a round of single crochet stitches over the ring until it is completely covered.

2 Join with a slip stitch to the first stitch. Break off the yarn, leaving an end of about 12 inches (30 cm) and thread it into a large yarn needle. Sew a row of running stitches around the edge of the crochet. Turning the edge of the crochet to the center of the ring, draw the thread up firmly and secure it.

3 On the back of the button, work strands of yarn diagonally across the button several times to make a shank. Sew the button on to the garment by sewing through the center of the strands.

APPLYING BEADS

Before starting to crochet, thread all the beads onto your ball of yarn. If you're using several balls to make a garment, for example, the pattern instructions will tell you how many beads to thread onto each ball of yarn. When choosing beads, match the size of the holes in the beads to the thickness of your yarn; small beads are best on fine yarns, and larger beads on chunky yarns. When working with different bead colors arranged in a particular pattern, don't forget that you should thread the different bead colors onto the yarn in reverse order, so the pattern will work out correctly as you crochet. Beads are nearly always applied on wrong side rows.

BEADING WITH SINGLE CROCHET

I Work to the position of the first bead on a wrong side row. Slide the bead down the yarn until it rests snugly against the right side of your work.

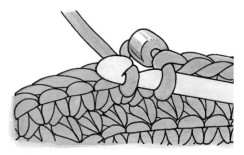

2 Keeping the bead in position, insert hook in next stitch and draw yarn through so there are two loops on the hook.

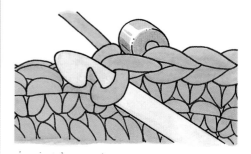

3 Wrap the yarn over the hook again and draw it through to complete the stitch. Continue adding beads in the same way across the row, following the pattern instructions.

APPLYING SEQUINS

Sequins can be applied to a background of single crochet in a similar way to beads. Round sequins are the best ones to use, either flat or cup-shaped types. As a general rule, thread sequins onto your yarn in the same way as beads.

When crocheting with cup-shaped sequins, make sure you thread them onto the yarn so the convex side of each sequin faces the same way toward the ball of yarn. When crocheted, the "cup" should face away from the crochet fabric, in order to show the sequin from the best advantage and to prevent the sequin damaging the crochet.

ADDING SEQUINS TO SINGLE CROCHET

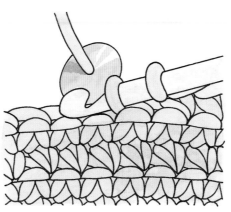

1 Work to the position of the first sequin on a wrong side row. Work the first stage of the single crochet, leaving two loops on the hook. Slide the sequin down the yarn until it rests snugly against the right side of your work. Remember, if you're using cup-shaped sequins, the convex side (the bottom of the "cup") should be next to the fabric.

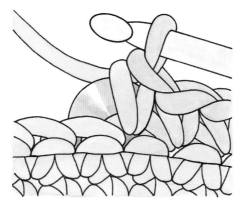

2 Keeping the sequin in position, wrap the yarn round the hook and draw it through to complete the stitch. Continue adding sequins in the same way across the row, following the pattern instructions.

WEB RESOURCES

The Craft Yarn Council:
www.craftyarncouncil.com

The Crochet Guild of America:
www.crochet.org

SELECTED SUPPLIERS
www.buy-mail.co.uk
www.coatscrafts.co.uk
www.colourway.co.uk
www.coolwoolz.co.uk
www.designeryarns.uk.com
www.diamondyarns.com
www.ethknits.co.uk
www.e-yarn.com
www.handworksgallery.com
www.hantex.co.uk
www.kangaroo.uk.com
www.karpstyles.ca
www.knitrowan.com
(features worldwide list of stockists of Rowan yarns)
www.knittersdream.com
www.knittingfever.com
www.knitwellwools.co.uk
www.lacis.com
www.maggiescrochet.com
www.mcadirect.com
www.patternworks.com
www.patonsyarns.com
www.personalthreads.com
www.letsknit.com
www.shetland-wool-brokers-zetnet.co.uk
www.sirdar.co.uk
www.spinningayarn.com
www.theknittinggarden.com
www.upcountry.co.uk
www.yarncompany.com
www.yarnexpressions.com
www.yarnmarket.com

MEASURING GAUGE

Most crochet patterns recommend a "gauge." This is the number of stitches (or pattern repeats) and rows to a given measurement (usually 4 inches or 10 cm). For your work to be the correct size, you must match this gauge as closely as possible. To work out a design of your own, you need to measure your gauge to calculate the stitches and rows required.

The hook size recommended by any pattern or ball band is only a suggestion. Gauge depends not only on the hook and yarn but also on personal technique.

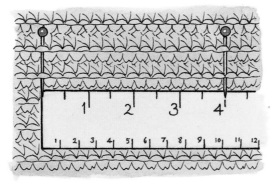

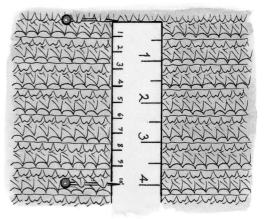

1 Work a piece of crochet about 6 inches (15 cm) square, using the hook, yarn, and stitch pattern required. Only press if this is recommended on the ball band. Lay the sample flat and place two pins 4 inches (10 cm) apart along the same row, near the center. Count the stitches (or pattern repeats) between them.

2 Then place two pins 4 inches (10cm) apart on a vertical pattern line near the center, and count the number of rows between them.
If you have too many stitches (or pattern repeats) or rows to 4 inches (10 cm), your work is too tight; repeat the process with another sample made with a larger hook. If you have too few stitches (or pattern repeats), or rows, your work is too loose; try a smaller hook. It is usually more important to match the number of stitches exactly, rather than the number of rows.

BLOCKING

Crochet often needs to be blocked before assembly, to "set" the stitches and give a professional finish.

Always follow the guidance given on the ball band, as some fibers can be spoiled by heat and moisture.

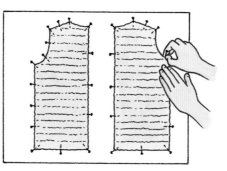

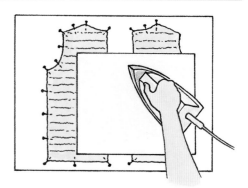

1 Lay each piece right side down on a well-padded surface. With rows straight, pin the pieces in place; inserting pins evenly all around at right angles to the edges. If necessary, ease the piece gently to size, checking the measurements. (Matching pieces, such as the two garment fronts shown here, may be pinned out side by side).

2 Check the yarn band for pressing instructions. For natural fibers, such as wool or cotton, a clean damp cloth and a warm iron are usually suitable. Lift and replace the iron lightly, do not rub. Leave to cool and dry completely before removing the pins. After assembly, press the seams gently.

Some yarns (such as some synthetics) should not be pressed: pin out the work as above, mist with cold water, and leave to dry.

AMERICAN/ENGLISH TERMINOLOGY

The patterns in this book use American terminology. Patterns published using English terminology can be very confusing because some English terms differ from the American system, as shown below:

AMERICAN	ENGLISH
single crochet (sc)	double crochet (dc)
extended single crochet (exsc)	extended double crochet (exdc)
half double crochet (hdc)	half treble crochet (htr)
double crochet (dc)	treble crochet (tr)
treble crochet (tr)	double treble crochet (dtr)
double treble crochet (dtr)	triple treble crochet (trtr or ttr)

CROCHET AFTERCARE

It is a good idea to keep a ball band from each project you complete as a reference for washing instructions. Crochet items are best washed gently by hand and dried flat, to keep their shape. Crochet garments should not be hung on coat hangers, but folded and stored flat, away from dust, damp, heat, and sunlight. Clean, acid-free tissue paper is better than a plastic bag.

STANDARD CROCHET ABBREVIATIONS

ch(s)	chain(s)	sk	skip
sl st	slip stitch	yo	wrap yarn over hook
sc	single crochet	rem	remaining
exsc	extended single crochet	cont	continue
hdc	half double crochet	alt	alternate
dc	double crochet	beg	beginning
tr	treble crochet	foll	following
dtr	double treble crochet	patt	pattern
st(s)	stitch(es)	RS	right side
sp(s)	space(s)	tog	together
lp(s)	loop(s)	WS	wrong side
rep	repeat		

INDEX

CREDITS

All photographs and illustrations are the copyright of Quarto Publishing plc.

ACKNOWLEDGMENTS

With thanks to DMC Creative World for kindly supplying many of the yarns used in this book:

DMC threads distributed in the USA by:
The DMC Corporation
South Hackensack Avenue
Port Kearny Bldg. 10F
South Kearny, NJ 07032-4688
Phone: 973-589-0606 for details of nearest stockist
or visit www.dmc-usa.com

Thanks also to Emily Hayden